MEN
PIGS

AND DESERVE TO DIE!

By Sonya Steinem

THUNDERBOLT PRESS
Suite #178
4001 S. Decatur
Las Vegas, Nevada 89103

Men Are Pigs
And Deserve To Die

By Sonya Steinem

Art Director: Farzi Hulan

Illustrated by Tani Johnson

THUNDERBOLT PRESS

Suite #178
4001 S. Decatur
Las Vegas, Nevada 89103

ISBN: 0-929-256-20-4

Library of Congress

This Book Is Dedicated To
Jane and Sally
Who Were Abused and Mistreated
By Dick and Spot
And Every Other Male
They Ever Knew

ABOUT THE AUTHOR

Sonya Steinem is a Stanford Phi Beta Kappa, single working mother, neurosurgeon, tennis pro, part-time model/pop singer, and concert pianist dedicated to saving dolphins, women and all other humble creatures from extinction.

The world acclaimed author of more than a dozen books of fiction and non-fiction, her current hobbies include skydiving, the triathalon and reading treatises on particle physics and gauge theory. Sonya is, alas, a typical modern woman.

CONTENTS

PART III: LIVING WITH YOUR PIG

PART IV: ALL MEN ARE PIGS

PART V: LIST OF NON-PIGS

INTRODUCTION

"Sonya," my dear colleagues have often begged of me, "Why don't you write a book to help others the way you've helped us?

I've touched thousands through my speaking engagements devoted to exploring the intimate question of why *Men Are Pigs*, but women throughout the civilized world are still clamoring, "Why don't you reach out to all of us and tell it like it really is?"

So, at the behest of oppressed women everywhere starved for my message, I have finally heeded the call and after calm measured reflection am most humbly offering this slim volume of the gods' honest truth:

Men Are Pigs And Deserve to Die!!!

But before we get into the sordid details that have led me and multitudes of other women to this conclusion, I must make a small disclaimer about the phrase "*Deserve To Die*." Lest any feeble-minded, spineless wonder of a pigish male misconstrue any of the factually based opinions held in this book as the random ravings of a hostile woman, understand that I, Sonya Steinem, do not condone violence whatsoever. Nor do I approve of negativity on any level, as a matter of fact. Au contraire, it is my intent that the women who read this oevre (and men, too, if any of you lame-brains would ever read a serious book for a change instead of confusing *"oevre"* with *"ovary"*), will come away with a message of overriding love.

The best way I can attempt to explain the volatile phrase -- "*Deserve to Die*" -- is to give the famous example of the *Figure of Death* as represented in the ancient art of *Tarot*. Whenever the Figure of Death shows up in a reading, it is never indicative of an actual death. Rather, it is a sign that inner and total transformation are imminent.

In other words, I'm not suggesting that men *should die*, but a lot of times men *ought to die* for their unconscionable behavior. Even though women may sometimes wish that men would "inhale a beer pull-tab and croak", what we really need is for these pigs to face up to their inadequacies and start to do something about them!!!

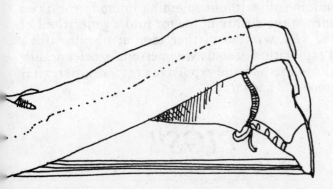

Yes, as kooky as it sounds, it is possible to love a pig, and for a pig to love back. As long as he's dealt with his payback!

As we join together to look at the many ways men (a.k.a. pigs) have stomped on women's innocence and ignored their superiority throughout the ages, it will become clear how males (sometimes masquerading as women, i.e. Maggie Thatcher) have managed to sell us a lethal, insidious bill of goods. We have been brainwashed by the macho male media into thinking that the following problems are feminine self-creations:

- Loving too much.
- Seeking out abusive men.
- Co-dependency and other addictions.
- Putting our lives and careers on hold for stupid swine who exist at the lowest level of the biological chain.
- Developing PMS and other strictly feminine emotional devices simply to torture men.

And ironically, the best these various authorities can offer by way of advice is to suggest that women are the ones who should change (I assume male publishers get a kick out of printing such tripe!).

Pleeeze! The hogwash has got to come to an end!

This explains why it has fallen to me, Sonya Steinem, your average ordinary regular kind of gal, to set the record straight. I am not a psychologist. I am not a New Age guru. I have no political platform or "hidden agenda" to prove. But, like the overwhelming majority of today's female population, *I've been to hell and back in a handbag!* and have miraculously lived to tell about it.

I feel I can speak from the sincere heart of womandom and, without sounding immodest, make a difference in the quality of life for future generations of women. So, without further ado, let's begin with a candid exploration of some very personal stories dealing with those loathed and repulsive creatures, hereafter understood and known as:

PIGS!!

PART I

SWINE SONG

1

DESCENT INTO HELL

Just When You Thought You Knew Them All!

Women, you've no doubt heard or experienced the following story before. In fact, you're probably living an inglorious hell just like it at this very moment!

The scenario is always the same: a young, vivacious, glamorous damsel whose life is filled only with spectacular promise has a sudden moment of weakness, brought on by fleeting loneliness and the latest *How-To-Catch-A-Man* article in **Cosmopolitan**. Inevitably, she falls prey to the machinations of some fast talking insect in a *Prince Charming* disguise who proceeds to run her ragged.

After the aforementioned cute but remorseless *Tomato Slug* has used and abused her, chewed her up and spat her out in little pieces, she realizes that he's failed to make good on his flowery promises. Where are his so-called storehouses of diamonds? How about that chateau on the Riviera he said he'd inherited from his ailing grandmother? But worse, instead of upholding his pledges of undying devotion and perpetual adoration, he has managed to completely ruin, obliterate, and otherwise destroy the life of a beautiful and kindhearted woman who's given her all to this slovenly jerk.

And yet, instead of nailing him to the cross of unfulfilled dreams and making him pay for his atrocities, our invincible heroine perseveres. To support the four or more children he tricked her into having, she works two or three jobs, trudging cheerfully along to keep not only her babies from starving, but also to support the millstone and pay off his assorted IRS and gambling debts.

BELIEVE IT OR NOT, I, SONYA STEINEM, WAS ONCE THAT VERY WOMAN UNTIL AT LONG LAST, I BROKE THE CHAINS THAT BOUND ME TO A DEGENERATE PIG AND HE GOT HIS PAYBACK!

Before The Fall

It all started out so brightly. There I was -- a first year medical student at Stanford, ace tennis star on the professional circuit, as well as the *Ford Agency's* hottest high fashion model. While my primary focus was neurosurgery, I was also in the middle of designing and launching a fabulous line of lingerie to be marketed in Japan. As you might expect, I was hard at work adding Japanese to the other five languages in which I am fluent.

A WORD OF CAUTION: IDLE HANDS MAKE FOR THE DEVIL'S PLAYGROUND.

My downfall came because one night I happened to have knocked off all my homework a month early. After playing around with an intricate matrix inversion of a chemical process and programming it into my computer, I found myself with nothing to do.

Suddenly a memory of my teenage days as a femme fatale wafted upon me. I was beset by the recollection of balmy summer nights when I would cruise exclusive San Francisco restaurants, mercilessly teasing an array of young executives before I crushed their hearts.

Men knew better than to mess with me. I was cold as ice.

Oh sure, I'd been around the block once or twice. I'd known a pig or two, even at my tender age. But I thought I knew the warning signs and how to avoid those lascivious dolts. Hah! That was my first mistake. In my state of overblown hormonal exuberance, I lacquered myself with my flashiest midnight-blue sequined evening dress, jumped on my Kawasaki 750, popped a few wheelies, and before long was pulling up to *Michelle's* -- one of my old favorite haunts.

Little did I realize as I sauntered into the place that by the end of the night I would be dragged down a slippery slope to Hades!! What was I thinking?!?!

His Name Was Steve...

I remember gasping when I saw him standing there at the bar with three vapid "*babes*" (that's what he called them) hanging all over him. As his and every other male head turned in my direction (my entrances were always exquisite), I checked him out. He was prime meat on the hoof: dark, handsome, six foot plus, dressed immaculately in a tuxedo, his Mediterranean eyes burning hot intelligence.

Instantly, I fell in love -- unthinking, stupid, wayward, misguided, ill-fated love!

He dropped the babes (literally, as the three tumbled to the floor) and strode smoothly over to my table, his deep voice murmuring in my ear:

"How'd'ya' like to buy me a drink, babe?"

Only in retrospect did I wonder if that could have been a shadow of things to come.

Steve, that was his name. Steve on the dotted line, Steve in slacks, Steve in the garden, Steve of my loins, and everything else Nabokovian. . . . Steve! ! !

We had nothing in common, but that didn't stop me from becoming his intimate amour. Sure, I knew I was turning a blind eye to his less than acceptable traits, but like foolish women the world over, *I thought I could change him!*

Hah ! ! !

Okay, so he was a piano mover for *Freedo's Moving and Storage* and hence the reason for the tuxedo (since he'd just come from working a wedding) that night we first met. Okay, so I thought at least he'd stay physically fit. So what if his specialty was moving pianos and mine was neurosurgery? Who cared that he was into watching football highlights while my hobbies were reading Proust and writing Haiku? Did it really matter that his greatest ambition was to one day own a corner bar and that mine was to become ambassador to the Soviet Union? Ah, those were the glory days of our relationship!

"*Sonya, you're the most beautiful woman in the world,*" he'd say to me and I would sigh innocently. It was only much later that I discovered he was quoting directly from his copy of the classic *HOW TO CATCH A WOMAN WHILE SHE'S STILL BREATHING.*

"*I'll do anything to please you!*" He'd promise.

In a pig's eye he would! ! !

But, tragically, I fell for it. I must have been hallucinating, I really believed that there were still men of grace and honor left in this world. How was I to know that although, upon my urging, Steve went back to get his high school diploma or though he brought me flowers now and then (plucked from the neighbor's garden) that this didn't a heaven-sent man make? I just got carried away thinking it was all so cute.

Then the goofball got me pregnant!

"How could you do this to me?!?!" Steve shouted, as if it was an immaculate conception.

"I thought you said you were infertile," I reminded him, unaware that he was dyslexic and used the word in place of "unfaithful," which he, in fact, was. As it turned out, Steve thought birth control was achieved by a wish and a prayer (*I wish I'd brought some protection and I pray to god she doesn't get pregnant!*).

SO MUCH FOR GOOD INTENTIONS AND MALE FORESIGHT!

"But, Steve," I implored him, practically in tears, "I thought you said you loved me!"

"*Of course I do l--o--o...*(unintelligible snort) *you,*" he responded already having trouble with the "L" word. *"But you know how much I need my freedom in order to bring out the creative passions that drive me! A baby might not fit into my lifeplan!"*

"My ass it won't fit into your lifeplan!" I almost screamed in unladylike passion, "I'll rearrange your lifeplan so you can sing soprano at the Met!" But I was sane enough to hold my tongue.

"I know it will be hard on you," I said instead. "But Steve, it will all work out fine. We're soulmates!"

You see, it was Steve's use of the word "creative" that had set my heart aflutter, distorting my better senses which should have informed me, had I been more observant, that Steve's creative passions had just gotten him fired from Freedo's for making a pass at the manager's wife. Newly employed by *Sneakers Galore*, a woman's jogging shoe outlet, Steve's latest creativity was limited to trying to get a gander up the culottes of "tennis chicks" (as he called them derisively).

Let me interrupt my tale briefly with some pertinent advice. Men are trained at birth to know exactly what our soft spots are, but their silver tongues are more forked than a rattlesnake's. So, ladies, be on the lookout for any of the manipulative double talk that follows:

Famous Phrases in Pig Latin

"You know, my CREATIVE PASSIONS are at war with my ROMANTIC NATURE, and you are the BATTLEFIELD OF MY SOUL!"

"My one fault is that I've always been an overly SENSITIVE human being."

"Most women think I'm more PHILOSOPHICAL than, uh, ahem, ah... NIETZCHE, but actually I'm more into HEMINGWAY and SPIELBERG!"

"Honey, you just make me so HORNY!"

Yessiree, Pig Latin will scramble your brains every time. Beware! But what's even scarier is that it is literally impossible for men to express certain phrases in Pig Latin, so you must also fine tune your instincts to words these hogsbreaths are unable to articulate. Words like:

- THE "L" WORD – *Love*
- THE "C" WORDS -- *Commitment and Caring*
- THE "M" WORDS – *Marriage, Matrimony, and Monogamy*
- THE "F" WORDS -- *For better or For worse and Foreplay*

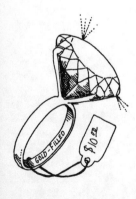

In any event, my Steve finally dealt with our predicament like a man: the next thing you know he's slipping this massive cubic zirconium engagement ring on my finger and saying, *"Sonya, I can't live without you."*

And he wasn't lying either since he'd put off his creditors (Tony the Shark, et al...) by telling them he was getting married and had a baby on the way.

Sure, this wasn't the exact replica of how I'd always dreamt love should be, but I decided to be patient, thinking without question that once we legalized our love bonds, Steve would soon fulfill his real potential.

I must have had a brain tumor!

Sonya's Wedding Album

Me and my bridal party. Sadly, Steve's Neanderthal buddies only had time to proposition fifteen year old Andrea twelve times before the ginger-ale-and-Ripple champagne ran out.

Steve and the "*Wild Boars*" on his side of the family. The guy in the polyester suit dragging Steve up the alter is his Uncle Burt, whose wife Agnes had him spayed after five strapping young piglets.

Sonya's Wedding Album

That's my mom at the reception, impaling herself on the ice sculpture as she cried, "*He's not good enough for you, my little Sonya!*"

Uncle Burt tried to show his concern by telling me, "So, our Stevie got you knocked up, what a kidder he is." Just after that, Burt pinched me on the rear, winked, and told me, "I sure hope you can cook better than you can put your makeup on, 'cuz Steve's real fussy!"

Here's me tossing the bouquet to that sad soul, Ethyl Brandywort, who shrieked and fainted when she realized she was next in line to walk the plank.

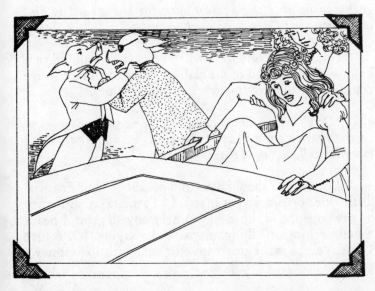

This is me, squeezing into Steve's fire-engine red Porsche that he informed me he was able to afford from having worked overtime at *SNEAKERS GALORE* (yeah sure!). Steve was having some ugly last words with his best man (curiously he'd chosen Tony the Shark).

Horror Honeymoon

As the drunken debauchery back at the wedding reception receded into the night, Steve and I sped off down the road to what I imagined was going to be a luxurious, pampering honeymoon, bidding Tony the Shark a fond farewell as he chased after us (brandishing a pistol and shouting obscenities).

I was just a tad disappointed when Steve explained that we were not heading towards any of the glamorous locations he'd originally promised, such as:

- **Tahiti**
- **Aruba**
- **Paris and the Riviera**
- **Detroit**

"*Nah,*" Steve said as we followed the roadsigns through god forsaken desert towards Las Vegas and the bowels of the earth, "*I got a new way to count cards and I'm going to be able to pay you back for the wedding and honeymoon with all my blackjack winnings!*"

I was mildly unsettled when he next announced that he'd turned over all of his cash to Tony the Shark so we could escape the wedding without bodily injury.

"*Don't worry Sonya-cakes, all we need is just a small cash advance from your credit cards and my gambling expertise will land us in the lap of luxury.*"

"Stevie, you should have told me about your financial difficulties before we got married," I remarked. But after he gave me one of those disarmingly boyish grins, I heard myself writing off all my misgivings by saying, "Of course I trust you to make smart investments with the money I give you because I love you. . ."

Before I was able to complete my optimistic thoughts, I looked up to see the delapidated marquee of the *MAL O' MAR MOTEL*, rated *XXXX, our honeymoon hideaway*. By the time Steve returned with the room key, I had fainted dead away, an event he attributed to my pregnancy.

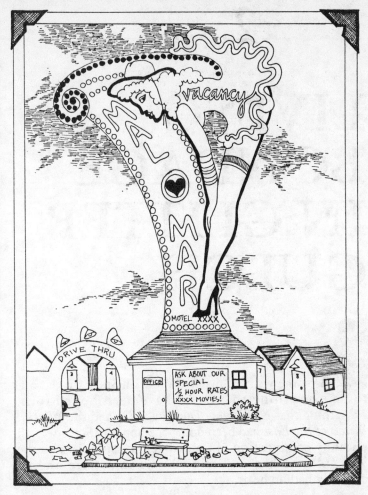

Yegads! Rates in the Mal O'Mar's deluxe *Norman Bates Honeymoon Suite and Lovenest* were by the hour!

When I revived, one short week later, Steve had completely wiped out my credit cards as well as my once ample savings account. He'd also lost the Porsche by betting it all on "*Old Swayback*" to win in the ninth at Santa Anita. Imagine my schizoid shock when I discovered that Steve had gotten me a job as a scullery maid at the *MAL O' MAR so now we wouldn't have to starve to death*.

But believe me you, the honeymoon was just the tip of the iceberg, Steve and I were a marital *Titanic* steaming boilers full into oblivion!

2

LIVING BONDAGE IN GLITTER GULCH

Living With Your *Pig!*

My nine years of married life with Steve turned out to be everything that could have been hoped for... everything that is, if I were *Dorothy of Oz* and the *Wicked Witch of the East* had been doing the hoping. Steve was an uncanny combination of the *Scarecrow*, the *Lion* and the *Tin Man*; he had no brains, he was a coward and he certainly had no heart.

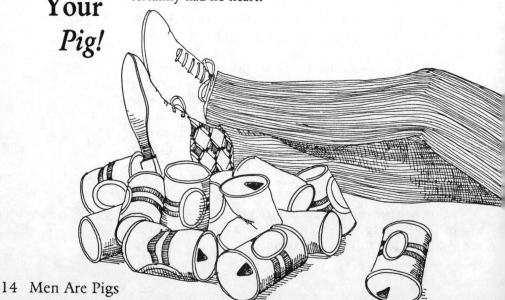

While other women might complain that their husbands are non-communicative, Steve seemed quite adept at maintaining a non-stop delivery of witty repartee:

- *"Looks like you're putting on some weight, Sonya-cakes. Sure doesn't look like cellu-LITE, looks more like cellu-FAT to me! Ha! Ha! Ha!"*
- *"Are the shutters flapping in the wind or is that your thighs slapping together?"*
- *"Hey, did you get bit by a couple of mosquitos? Oh, I'm sorry, those are your knockers!"*
- *"Ugh, do I smell tuna? Oh, it's you, dear. I didn't see you come in!"*
- *"Snort, snort, belch, burp, scratch, scratch, snort, belch. Ha! Ha! Ha!"*

To make a long story short, it took many years for the proverbial pieces of the enigmatic puzzle called Steve to finally fit together. Besides, I was too busy contributing to our welfare to accurately size up the situation. In addition to my back-breaking household duties as washerwoman, scrub sergeant, ironing technician, appliance repairperson, etc..., I was also occupied with raising our four children: Spike, Scooter and Sluggo (you guessed it, Steve named them) and baby Sally, my pride and joy.

In my spare time, I worked as a night maid at one of the local hotels (which was a real breeze compared to the

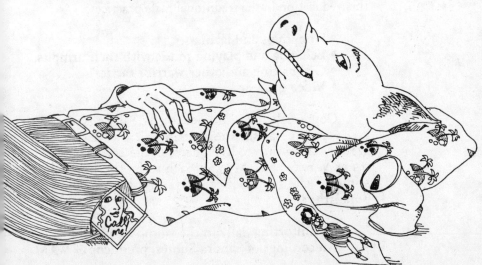

kind of mess I handled at home) and held down a part-time job as a secretary at *HARROLD'S USED MATTRESS EMPORIUM.* Eventually, after Harrold made a pass at me right under his wife's nose and I barely got out of there with my clothes on, I got better working conditions as a secretary at a nearby convent and they even helped me with my legal expenses later on. Somehow, I even managed to volunteer my services for two important charities, attend night classes in accounting, do the household finances, keep the VW running, and at least attempt to retain my girlish figure.

Who me? A domestic martyr? You're damn straight!!!

Steve's duties were to keep track of both the baseball **AND** the football scores.

"What happened to the fun girl I used to know? Boy have you changed!" Steve was very perceptive. What a guy! What a pig!

I should also confess that Steve did lend a hand every now and then in the upbringing of Spike, Scooter and Sluggo, who he was determined to raise as smudged little carbon copies of himself. Ergo, despite my deep love for the little tykes, they became stupid, obnoxious, filthy, rude miniature male hellions cut from the same cookie mold as their father. Steve took meticulous measures to ensure their education in the traditional male practices:

- Sloppiness and laziness.
- Belching and playing music with their armpits.
- Girl baiting and other warrior tactics.
- Video games.

Conversely, I decided not to give Sally a typical little girl's training as she most definitely was destined to a greater calling than to live a decrepit life as a packmule for some *Neanderthal.* My approach to mothering included some of the techniques only now gaining national popularity:

- Comforting Sally in the womb by playing recordings of Sandra Shores, president of WAM

(Women Against Men), screaming obscenities at the male species full volume.

- Giving her a mantra at aged two: "Men are no good" I'd coo and baby Sally would reassuringly echo, "Mem No Gooo."
- Forgoing the dolls and teacups for more sophisticated toys such as a battery operated water-pistol which I instructed her to aim only at the opposite sex.

"Shoot 'em right between the eyes Sally," I'd suggest as we cruised the Vegas strip and she'd hang out the window shouting "Mem no goo" with the water-pistol spraying wildly.

In some ways, I suppose, marriage to Steve was as average and all-American as apple pie.

Every apple rotten to the core!

Without question life did have its lighter, funnier moments. Like the time I took five days off to go visit my sister in Phoenix and came back to find Steve with the engine to the VW on the kitchen table, the carburetor sitting in the collander in the sink and the pistons holding down broken plates in the dishwasher. . .

What a crack-up!

Or then there was the time Steve invited his dwarf half-brother *Elron* and wife *Moonchild* for lunch and they wound up staying the whole summer. What a laugh riot! Although a lesser woman might have been inconvenienced by having to feed and dress these *Druids* and their two hell-spawned kids -- *Spacechild* and *Son of Elron* -- and then abide the yapping of *Bandito*, their pernicious little shaved *Chihuahua* who didn't shut up for three months, I felt that the intellectual stimulation provided by intense discussions with Elron about the socio-economic implications of the impending *Harmonic Divergence* more than made up for the added stress.

It still brings tears to my eyes!

I guess what really started to bug me about Steve was something a bit more intangible than the minor irritations

of life. It wasn't the fact that he was irresponsible and incompetent at doing anything other than popping beer can tabs, or that he'd never learned how use anything more complicated than a spoon at the dinner table. Nor did it upset me when he insisted that women were *stupid!!* and that he, an uneducated boor, was always right.

No, what really chapped my butt was when he started to get caught up in the masculine *Bright Ideas Syndrome!* I'm certain all you women out there know what I'm talking about and could add extensively from your own pig's portfolio to this list of *Steve's Bright Ideas for getting rich without actually working*:

- First there was the crash and burn blackjack scheme that left us threadbare and stranded in Las Vegas.
- Then there was another project he swore would make us a mint: Steve (all by himself!) re-invented the square yo-yo.
- Likewise, he designed and patented a recliner with a television remote built into the arm rest as well as a pulley system for opening the fridge and extracting a six-pack.

- A ten thousand dollar **Computer Dynamics at Home** course approved by veterans (con veterans, I'm sure) that allowed Steve to play Pac-Man and Nintendo almost as well as his sons Spike and Scooter, although he beat Sluggo regularly.

It's kind of incredible the way **Bright Ideas** can add up and pretty soon you've mortgaged the house five times over to support pie-in-the-sky dreams that never bring in one cent of revenue while time just drifts on by because you're having so much fun. So I kept my jobs and Steve kept trying to make us rich. It must go back to genetics, because doesn't it seem to you that only men are capable of **Bright Ideas** while we girls are only capable of doing the mop-up when the party is over?!

And for the entire nine years Steve never once agreed to take out the garbage! He was a total and complete PIG!!!

But what was I complaining about? Over and over, I reassured myself that I'd married the American dream. I had a handsome (albeit philandering and sodden) husband, one out of four charming children, and though I was pushing thirty I had kept my weight well below two hundred pounds. Hadn't those younger visions of Tahiti, neurosurgery, Nobel Prizes, a meaningful existence. . . been just silly illusions, monstrous perversions of reality?

Listen, sisters, if you think for one second that I was satisfied with my male dominated, fascist oppressive existence, having the lifeblood sucked out of me by this male leech, then you're as duped as I once was !!

I was ready for murder and mass mayhem, for destruction and revolution. But unlike those imbecellic, slothful male creatures who'd been a pox upon my very existence, I wanted to accomplish my revenge like a lady, in a refined, dignified, well-dressed and genteel fashion. I wanted to hold my head high in a male dominated world and be proud as the divine, feminine being that I am, serene and complete in the knowledge of my innate superiority.

In other words, I wanted to rip Steve's cold and unfeeling heart out of his body with my bare hands so that he would know what I meant when I swore that the payback was going to be a bitch! ! ! !

3

LAST
STRAWS

As I later told the prosecutor, with tearful eyes and a choke in my voice, it wasn't premeditated murder at all, it was self-defense!!

When The Camel's Back Snaps!

Let me state the facts as objectively as is humanly possible and allow you to judge for yourself.

"Hey Sonya, let's have another kid!" Steve began the inhuman taunting that would soon become more than sanity could bear.

"What'd you do while I was out looking for work, watch Donohue for eight hours, or just eat bon-bons? Ha! Ha! Ha!"

It had been over a year since Steve had been employed, yet he still had the nerve to question me about my one day off from working my regular two jobs. It was apparent that Steve had begun a maniacally conceived plan of abuse that was destined to drive me to chaos. It continued with his daily refusal to take out the trash, followed quickly by another one of his familiar tricks: leaving a half empty *Coors* in little Sally's crib.

I can't even remember half the odious things that Steve said to me that night. As I staggered through the living room to pick up after him, sweeping up the tonnage of beer cans, digging the mounds of crushed potato and

corn chips from out of the carpet, scouring the pizza sauce stains off the sofa, a pressing question suddenly overpowered me.

Where had I left the Dust Buster?!

Don't ask me why I thought to look in Steve's make-shift tool shed (made with his own skilfull hands out of scrap plywood and spare engine parts) but sure enough, there was the dustbuster, lying amidst old *Playboys* and a virtual *Banana Republic* arsenal of exotic weaponry.

Have you ever noticed how most men aren't satisfied with having one gun for their hunting jaunts? Steve, it seemed, required an AR-15 assault rifle (which conveniently converted into a military M-16 machine gun), an Ingram M-10 semiautomatic, a double-barrel Derringer, a shotgun, a two foot hunting knife, a pen gun, a pair of nunchuks, a machete, a Beretta 9mm pistol, some smoke bombs and these razor edged karate-ninja throwing stars.

All of this just so he could go out and shoot Bambi!!!

Being that I'm a well-respected lover of animals and a pacifist, you might wonder how I was able to identify the above-mentioned weapons of death and/or their manufacturers. Honestly, I must stress that I hardly knew their names, much less how to use them. But I'd also like to interject that if you ever come across an Ingram M-10 you should really weld two ammo clips together or you're going to run out of bullets too fast!

Wait, I'm getting ahead of myself. You see, Steve also had a stack of **SOLDIER OF MAYHEM** magazines which (since I happen to be a speed reader) I was able to review carefully in a matter of ten minutes.

I never thought in my wildest nightmares that I'd actually come to use any of these despicable firearms, so you'll agree that I must have succumbed to momentary amnesia when I took a fast drive over to the **Mercenary Gun Store** to purchase a camouflage outfit.

Ladies, in case you ever are in the market for a camouflage ensemble, let me remind you that there is little variety in what's available as far as size, color,

fabric, and especially style. So, if you're a smart shopper, like me, you can't go wrong by walking the extra mile for complimentary matching accessories to be found at reasonable prices at your local K-Mart and other fine department stores or pawn shops.

In my case, I was fortunate enough to find an exquisite *Gucci* knock-off carry-all, coordinating it with an adorable silk scarf, "fishing spinner" earrings, an imitation Puka shell necklace, and my favorite lipstick: *Cherries in the Snow.*

Sure, the fact that I went to such lengths to look good when I felt like *hell* might make my little outburst with Steve seem as if it were planned. But I swear that I don't remember really putting a *bonzai* strategy together until the following evening when Steve's criminal neglect rose to an all time high.

Armageddon

"*Is dinner ready?*" Steve bellowed at me as he opened the door so that I was able to notice Ethyl, his mistress, standing there behind him.

I slipped Ethyl, the poor thing, some money for cab fare back home and I turned on my heels, confusion racking my brain.

"*Monday Night Football's on and I've got a sure bet on Greenbay...*" Steve continued. Even I knew that Vince Lombardi's ghost wouldn't bet on Greenbay!

"*So bring me something to eat and don't disturb me.*"

Just then it occurred to me that maybe Steve was already disturbed.

"*Listen, Sonya, I'm leaving you for another woman. Your PMS and constant nagging are stifling my creativity. Her name is Peaches and the kids will like her a lot better. She's a Brazillian dancer at the Oba Oba show down at the Aladdin. I'm filing for divorce tomorrow and I guess you'll have to pay alimony cause I'm keeping the children.*"

IT WAS THAT SPLIT- SECOND THAT I CRACKED! THE FEAR THAT THE GARBAGE WOULD NEVER BE TAKEN OUT FOR THE REST OF GOD DAMN ETERNITY CONSUMED MY SENSES.

"Oh," was his next comment, *"Ethyl's just a business associate of mine, so don't give me any lip about her."*

Yes, some part of me had snapped and let me tell you it wasn't my bra strap!

I rounded up Sluggo, Scooter, Spike and Sally and sent them next door to the babysitter. Then I went upstairs and while Steve continued his eternal love affair with the boob tube, step by step, inch by inch, I began donning my camouflage attire, putting on my warpaint in an almost hypnotic ritual. When I finished with a final look in the mirror (Yes! I was still *exquisite!*), I headed for Steve's garage arsenal where I loadedup with all the artillery I could carry. With fire-sale excitement I filled the pockets of my combat fatigues with extra clips of ammunition and loaded up my **Gucci** knock-off carry-all with what I figured was enough explosives to cure every problem I had ever had with men.

"Honey, run down to the store and get me another sixer' and some damn dip for these chips before half-time is over. You're not mad at me are you?"

Me mad? No way!

I rammed home the clip in the M-16 and patted it fondly.

"Where'd you go Sonya? Can't I even watch a little football without you throwing one of your fits? The kids'll like Peaches, she's a lot more understanding than you are."

"It's all over Steve!" I replied, standing in the archway of the family room in full metal jacket. **"The payback's always a bitch!"** I spoke quietly, calmly, only the glint of a smile hinted by my *Cherries in the Snow* expression.

Sprawled on the couch and surrounded by strewn copies of centerfolds from Playboy, Penthouse, and Oui (which

Steve pronounced "*OOOO-weeee*") was the man of the hour. The room had been spotless only twenty minutes before, but now it was littered with beer cans, pizza crusts, and greasy globs of bean dip everywhere. Slowly, a light of began to dawn on Steve's face.

"*Does this mean you don't love me anymore?*" He asked unsurely.

I lowered the muzzle of the sawed-off shotgun, pumped once, and then let spew 8 ounces of hot scatter shot, silencing forevermore that inane banter that had tormented me all those years. The television exploded into a firey inferno as I sent *Monday Night Football* to an incandescent hell.

"*Sonya, I can see you're a little upset,*" Steve cautioned nervously, a faint glimmer of respect finally emerging in his glazed *Bud-Lite* eyes.

BOOM! BOOM! BOOM! Was my terse reply, as the shotgun ripped into Steve right where it hurt him worst: the cases of **Heidlebrau** he was saving for Superbowl Sunday spritzed and foamed into a bubbling Valhala.

*"Take a **Midol** or something,"* Steve sputtered and meekly added, *"I just know this is a bluff about the garbage, isn't it!? But you don't have the balls to point that gun at me and pull the trigger!"*

I discarded the spent shotgun, raised the Ingram M-10 and pointed it at Steve's head.

"EAT LEAD, PIG, AND DIE!!!!!!" I screamed, as I poured out ten rounds in a rapid tat-tat-tat succession.

MAYBE IT WAS A SUB-CONSCIOUS THING, BUT I SOMEHOW MANAGED TO MISS STEVE, EVEN AT THAT CLOSE RANGE. WAS I STILL IN LOVE?

Steve didn't lose that opportunity to ramble off towards the kitchen in search of cover. This is where all those years of exercising to Jane Fonda workout tapes and scrubbing floors paid off because Steve was as soft as the *Pillsbury Doughboy* while I was hardened sinews of steel ready for combat. In desperation, he began throwing his collection of international tupperware beer mugs at me, one of which bruised my shoulder, but I stood my ground and unleashed a clip from the M-16 that sent our sacred wedding china crashing to the floor. Then I charged, with the Ingram spraying Steve's path with dragon breath and me with the look of blood in my eyes.

DID THIS MEAN OUR MARRIAGE WAS IN TROUBLE?

There was still a chance for our relationship if only that nosewipe had begged for mercy and apologized for his insensitivity right there. Instead, Steve looked at me for an incredible instant that seemed to say he thought I was the one who was crazy!

That iced the cake!

As Steve rambled out of the kitchen and lumbered upstairs, I charged down the hall behind him screaming *PIGGG!!!* at the top of my lungs. With a *whirrr-zzzappp!* I caught him with a Ninja star in the butt before he reached the top and I heard him squeal in well deserved pain. Steve was really trying my patience now, but by the time I'd climbed the stairs to deliver the *coup de grace*, the numskull had locked himself into the bathroom.

What a wimp! What a pig!

"*Make peace with your maker, you slime,*" I yelled. "*The 82nd Airborne couldn't save you now!!*"

"*But what did I do? ! ? ! ?*"

Yes, those typically ludicrous male words were Steve's last, oinked just before I let loose a couple of hand-grenades, tossed a package of homemade C-4 explosives into the bathroom and ran for cover.

KABOOOOOOM !!!!!!!!!!

The force of the explosion literally tore half of the house off, pulverizing for good the lowlife **MAN** who'd made a mockery of me. I was free at last, *free at last, free at last !!!*

I had really hoped to have avoided bloodshed, but I'd been pushed over the brink by years of mental abuse. A woman can only put the toilet seat down 5 billion times before she finally cracks!!

The police never did find Steve's body (I wasn't surprised, I have yet to meet a man who could help with the cleanup after the party is over). Yet, I was somehow left saddened, and not because Steve had long ago hocked his life insurance premium on a fifty horsepower *John Deere* lawnmower/cat-mulcher now rusting in the back yard. No, for all his faults, Steve had once been the man of my dreams, but now he'd vaporized into thin air before he'd even gotten a chance to appreciate how much I really loved him.

"It's just like my aunt Bernice Bernstein used to say," I sobbed to the police lieutenant first on the scene, with a tear in my eye and a lump in my throat.

"REVENGE IS BEST SERVED COLD, BUT IT'S NOT BAD EVEN IF YOU BURN YOUR TONGUE!"

The Trial and Beyond

"Ladies and *gentlemen* of the jury," the male prosecutor solemnly intoned at my trial. "Surely you see that this *mankiller* woman is *psychotic, neurotic,* and *hopelessly twaddled* by the effects of *PMS* and a thousand other *mental frailties pe-cul-i-ar* to the *female species*." He almost gagged on the words "female species" before continuing.

"For the *unprovoked* slaughter of a *hardworking, caring* and *loving* husband, who deserved her *undying* respect and *grovelling devotion* until *death do us part,* we can only judge that she be *hung by her neck* until she turns *blue* and *croaks!*"

On the stand, though, I was able to paint a vivid picture of my own suffering.

"Sometimes, Steve would force me to watch football games **AND** football highlights for weeks on end!" I sobbed through heartfelt tears. "The psychological terror of having to endure Frank Gifford, Dan Dierdorf and Al Michels all those years was worse than being a *Vietnam War P.O.W.!*" And then I broke into full blown cries of anguish.

The women of the jury all nodded in agreement; their pig-dominated lives must have been as abominable as mine. Even the men squirmed in their seats, their eyes darting aside in guilt, knowing even as I spoke that they were no better than Steve. The final verdict was a unanimous decision and I was vindicated!

Men Are Pigs and Deserve to Die!!

I walked out of that courtroom a free woman, resolved to help women everywhere free themselves from male servitude.

"This is only the beginning!" I told the prosecutor after the trial. The poor schmuck was standing in the corridor crying in miserable defeat.

"NOW, IT'S OUR TURN TO DO THE HEARTBREAKING!!!"

My voice echoed triumphantly throughout the hallowed halls of justice and through the hearts and minds of a nation of oppressed women.

Before long, the kids and I were on our feet again. I completed my degree in neurosurgery and soon resumed my multiple careers. After all, I am woman and therefore naturally superior. Soon, I'd lost all that weight I'd gained as Steve's doormat, which in turn allowed me to get back on the professional tennis circuit and be welcomed back by the media to my high-fashion modeling career.

It was really true: merely associating with a slovenly man is a proven emotional and physical health risk. Gone were the headaches; gone were the arguments about who would take out the trash and whether or not I could have cats for pets. Life was a bed of roses again!

But don't let the happy ending to my story fool you. This was only one chapter in one woman's ordeal. After it was over, I realized that there were millions of other women struggling and clawing daily to cope with men who simply lacked the intelligence to comprehend deep concepts like *cleanliness* and *bargain shopping*.

The Women of the World needed me!

Yet, before I would be ready to help those other women, I first had to face some old pig skeletons in my own closet.

It's just so impossible to get rid of them!!!!

4

NAGGING QUESTIONS

Pig-men-to-sis (pig'men∗to∗sis) n. Biol. Condition afflicting women causing an acute attraction to and by swine-like men; often fatal. 2. Euphemism for love.

Measure The Pain!

Most women have the uneasy feeling that they too might be suffering from pigmentosis (sort of like walking around with an undiagnosed yeast infection). But can you quantify the pain and suffering you've experienced at the hands of that "special guy" in your life to be really sure you're not just a hypochondriac?

Yes, dear souls, yes! There is a way to measure the oppression **Mr. Potato-Head** has heaped on you all these years! No, it isn't in your mind or just some kind of *neurotic, PMS-induced* anxiety, you are *used* and *abused* and all it takes is a questionaire to prove it (better than the sex ones in **Cosmo!**). The following quizes employ the most advanced psycological testing methods available from Bryn Mawr college to make sure that all results will be fair and impartial and in no way biased against men simply because they're pigs.

QUIZ #1
The Ten Most Common Symptoms Of Pigmentosis

Rate Yourself. Check the statements that accurately describe your desperate male-oppressed situation:

_____1. When I pass a construction site and the men/animals whistle and cat-call, I don't care that these high-school dropouts earn more than me and my PhD !

_____2. I'm so desperate for love that it doesn't bother me that the weirdest geek in any crowd will inevitably seek me out and hit on me like a cruise missile!

_____3. I'm not at all embarrassed that every good-looking guy I've ever met (or married) turned out to have no job, no car and lived with his mother.

_____4. I believe I deserve to live in squalid poverty paid half as much as the mail boy.

_____5. I believe women's purpose is to live yoked to household labor as the human vessel for a man's seed.

_____6. I'm convinced childbirth is a pleasure cruise that should be counted as vacation time!

_____7. My favorite thing about men is that after spilling soup on their tie and making loud animal noises in lieu of saying, "*Pass the salt!*", they still think you're obligated to go to bed with them.

_____8. I'm flattered by disgusting skirt jokes like "Women should be obscene and not heard!"

_____9. As a woman, I don't think I'm entitled to orgasms, my own career, or a yacht.

_____10 The way I know my man loves me is that he forgets our anniversary, smells like a dead rat soaked in *Coors* and refers to me and the kids as "*crumb-snatchers*."

IF YOUR TOTAL IS:

ZERO -- Congratulations, at least you've escaped the terror-tactics of brainwashing afoot in our land. You'll benefit immensely from the suggestions that fill this book. I should, however, warn you that murdering a man is still considered a crime in some states.

ONE TO TEN -- Fear not. Although you're no doubt suffering from a severe case of pigmentosis, believe me when I say: It's not your fault! It's him, the pig!!!

Just to prove who's really to blame for the present warfare between the sexes, see how the male nitwit in your life scores on the next quiz.

Quiz #2
The Abuse Factor -- Rating Him

Estimate the frequency of the following events. When finished,
add up your score, noting the negative value of alternate questions:

— _____ 1. How often each day does he irritate you?

\+ _____ 2. Add the times each day he says he loves you and really means it!

— _____ 3. Subtract the number of times he's called you a broad, a chick, thunderthighs or accidently by some other woman's name (including his mother's!).

\+ _____ 4. Plus the number of pieces of valuable jewelry he's given you over the course of your miserable relationship.

— _____ 5. Less the times he's gotten whiplash watching platinum blonde women in tight leather mini-skirts sashay by.

\+ _____ 6. Plus the times in his life he's taken out the trash or done the wash without being asked.

— _____ 7. Minus the number of times a week he acts as if he's listening, but really ignores you because he thinks you're a fool.

\+ _____ 8. Add again the number of dinners plus flowers, plays, ballets and symphony concerts he's actually taken you to you since you've known him.

— _____ 9. Minus the number of times you've faked an orgasm to keep him from feeling impotent.

\+ _____ 10. Add the few times he's satisfied you in bed.

— _____ 11. Multiply the times he's cheated on you by 200 and subtract it fast before your blood boils!

\+ _____ 12 Add a little if he's really cute.

— _____ 13. But hack off the number of minutes he really is a *Pig!* and deserves to die!!!

— _____ 14. Show him no mercy! Lower the final count by the number of times he's laughed at *Andrew Dice Clay,* that hulking banana-brain!

TOTAL _____

IF HIS SCORE IS:

GREATER THAN ZERO -- Go back to second grade and learn how to add and subtract!

0 to -100 --- You're either a blessedly fortunate woman or you've cracked under the pressure and should redo the test with an objective friend in the midst of a bitter divorce.

-100 to -1000 -- This is the normal range for most women. Although bruised and abused, you're still breathing and should be thankful for that!

-1000 and below --- This is the pitiful state of martyrdom experienced by women who are the wives of politicians, preachers and billionaires (Lee Hart, Pat Nixon, Joan Kennedy, Ivana Trump and, heaven forbid, Tammy Baker).

As tragic as these telling statistics may reflect your current straits, the in-depth case studies next to come will at least let you know you are in good company:

With every woman in the world!

PART II

A PIG IS A PIG IS A PIG

5
THE ORIGINS OF MAN

Archaeological finds of ancient Sumerian clay tablets have recently been deciphered that explode Darwin's simplistic thesis that man evolved from the apes. While members of the old school held that since "God created man, it proves She has a sense of humor," authorities from the Vassar departments of anthropology, archaeology and theology have an updated view that is somewhat more complex.

Is God A Woman After All?

*According to my sources, the "**Sumerian Pig Sty Creation Story**" goes something like this:*

In the beginning, there was only a primordial slop, a planetary mush inhabited by creatures too foul and chaotic to even describe except to say that the lowliest amoeboid beings of all were called (you guessed it) **MEN!!**

Some many million years BC (before Cleopatra) the Goddess Mother of the Universe decided that CHAOS must be changed to ORDER and *She* began a massive home decorating project. In *Her* wisdom, *She* moved mountains here, rechanneled mighty rivers there and caused oceans to be made where before there had been none.

"Let there be Cosmic Enddust," *She* commanded. And there was.

"Let there be indoor-outdoor carpeting," *She* commanded. And there was.

"Let there be cute floral wallpaper," *She* added and, of course, there was.

Even the most grotesque of the resident creatures appreciated the Goddess Mother's decorative generosity, complimenting *Her* on *Her* fabulous taste. All the creatures, that is, except one.

This lower than urchinous creature was none other than the **MAN!!!!!!** creature, which, like the pond scum he was, delighted in befouling the new ORDER. He caused algal growths here, cess pools there and in general acted the role of ingrate in Paradise. It got so horrendous that the Goddess Mother was moved to cover everything in creation with something she called "plastic slip-covers."

In *Her* infinite patience and purest quality of love, the Goddess Mother would have abided the abominations of the scuzzy **Man** creature throughout eternity, except that he had acquired in his disevolutionary way the scheming gift of speech.

"*Heh babe, come on down and take a walk on the wild side,*" He'd gurgle. "*I know you're lonely and how do you know you won't like it unless you try it?*"

Knowing quite well that *She* could never consort with such a heinous creep, the Goddess Mother decided to try to change him into something more worthy than the gutter snipe he literally was.

Lo and behold: a deal was struck. *She* agreed that upon occasion *She* would allow the larva-like Man to visit her Heavenly Boudoir. But in return he was required to evolve into something more acceptable, anything which wouldn't spoil the interior decorating chore of an eternity.

"*Heh, toots, how's this?*" He'd spittle as he metamorphosed into a leech or a similar gelatinous invertebrate in a pathetic mockery of their holy agreement.

"Somehow, I think it lacks the proper dignity", She'd respond sweetly, softening the blow to his always fragile ego.

"*How's this, sugar? Pretty good, huh?*" He'd grin, flapping his leg flippers and slithering across the mud flats.

"No, not quite what I had in mind."

Nothing the hideous being had in stock appealed to the Goddess Mother who was wondering where this tormenting **MAN!!!!!!** creature had come from and how *She* could be rid of him. Perhaps, *She* thought, it would be best just to ignore him.

No dice, sisters! His next blasphemous request was even worse!

"*Heh, those are odacious balloons you got! How's about we get naked and do some mud wrestling?*"

"I'm sorry," *She* replied demurely, blushing several shades of the spectrum. "But it appears I'll be rolling my hair for a millenia or two." The Goddess Mother was always so polite, even to a creature who had grown legs and a tail and was now calling himself a "crocodile," whatever that is.

"*Now you've really hurt my feelings,*" said the crocodile, shedding tears. "*And after everything I've done for you!*"

"There, there, it's nothing personal," *She* comforted him, "But I feel a headache coming on, whatever that is, and wish to be alone for an eternity or two."

"*But baby, honey, doll, sweet-cakes,*" he argued, "*I'm so gooood for you!*" And then he changed into jackass form, braying and kicking up a celestial cloud of grime in a childish tantrum.

His protestations went on for aeons. From a jackass he evolved into a groundhog, then a legged worm, to a toothy snake and a weasel and countless other guises of unsavory appearance and dubious morals.

"**NO MORE!!!**" The Goddess Mother finally shrieked, dividing continents, upending the moons of Jupiter and altering the orbits of planets great and small. "Can't you pleeeez **GROW UP?!?!**"

For once, the **MAN!!!!!!** creature seemed to listen. Suddenly, his illbegotten amorphous mind and repulsive body began to change as a fireworks of all the glorious colors of the rainbow showered the earth.

She watched a miracle of creation unfold as he slowly but surely transformed into a normal HUMAN BEING!!! *She* beheld before *Herself* a kind and gentle, strong and caring creature, as handsome and complete as a galaxy of emotions that spanned all space and time. *He* reached out and touched the heart of the Goddess Mother as *She* had never been touched before.

An ecstasy gripped *Her* and spread like an ocean of happiness and love across the entire universe. And then, choked with feeling too powerful to express, *He* whispered to *Her* the one question that had tormented *Him* through the ages.

"Hey, toots, is there any beer in the cooler??"

"YOU PIGGGG!!!!!!!!!" She screamed!

And indeed, that is what *He* has been ever since.

6

THE INTELLIGENCE FACTOR

It's All In The Genes!

Some other plausible theories about men's innate inferiority come to us from leading psychologists and biologists. Perhaps the most popular of these is the suggestion that men are simply *genetically deficient*; i.e., they lack the better half of an **X Chromosome** which would otherwise allow them to engage in some sort of civilized behavior.

It's obvious, as the famous socio-endocrinologist Ragida Ormones pointed out to me, that since men's heads are not only physically bigger than women's, but also thicker, we're able to conclude that men are organically thick-headed. Oddly enough, male doctors regularly deny this observation.

Of course they do! It's because they too have fat heads composed almost entirely of calcium deposits and bone and are in no position to comment.

Especially gynecologists!!

Speaking of whom, every woman on the planet realizes that male OB-GYN's are a prime example of the axiom that **Men Are Pigs And Deserve to Die!** Only males could be brain impaired enough to think they know

more about female anatomy than women themselves. So why even go to a male gynecologist in the first place? It's like taking your car to a mechanic who's never owned one!

Lord! Men can't even fix the toilet plumbing around the house and then we're supposed to expect them to fix our own personal plumbing!?!?

And, by the way, why are gynecologists always short, nasal-congested, wormy types with lots of nervous ticks who look like Nazi war criminals or as though they've just been released from jail for performing immoral experiments on bunnies? I mean, most OB-GYNs are lucky if they know which end of the speculum to look through, much less remember what to look for once they get there. You might as well set an orangutang lose with a couple of cold soup spoons from the refrigerator as expect male idiots to figure out what's going on down in your lower forty!

Hypnotic Delays

Linguists and social workers who have long been studying masculine forms of communication postulate that the lag time between thought and verbalization is considerably slower among men.

In other words, although they think they're saying something truly profound, their words betray the fact that they're just plain dumb.

"Have you ever noticed how football is like life?"

How often have you heard that bit of oatmeal dribble from loverboy's cerebellum? It's as if men think the purpose of life is to wallow in mud, pat each other on the butt and whack their heads against steel goalposts until they can't see straight. But then, look what happens when you try to ask men a basic issue-related question such as:

"Herbert, do you think nuclear proliferation threatens complete global destruction, or do you perceive that small factions of survivors from such a holocaust would evolve to a higher consciousness and solve the problem of war for all time?"

"Yup," he'll reply.

WHAT THE HELL DOES "YUP" MEAN??!!

"Yup," according to specialists, is a man's primitive code for communicating that he thought about whatever question you've asked many years ago and that by scrupulous reasoning has deduced not only the exact answer to the problem, but also the values of the first five million *Fibonacci* numbers, their square roots and logarithmic corollaries, and now you've just bored him.

You've bored him!!!

Sadly, what "yup" really means is: "I've got a brain the consistency of bean curd and wouldn't know the answer to your question, even if I was listening, which I wasn't because my attention span is that of a two year old's and I ignore everything broads say no matter how brilliant it might be."

Sound familiar? You bet it does sister, but don't let these ruses fool you! Most of the illiterate ignoramuses can't even read the back of a cereal box, much less something as taxing as a book. My once husband Steve had a library that spanned all of four books:

- Conan the Barbarian
- Slave Girls of Gore
- The Story of O
- The Grinch that Stole Christmas

Of course, Steve didn't read very well but since he'd seen the Conan movie (that Scwartzeneggar, what a guy!) he bought the book as a memento. He also tried to get me to read out loud from *Slave Girls of Gore* and *The Story of O*, but I refused when I found out that only perverts like Steve and his *Bud-Lite* bonding-buddies could understand the sick things going on in them. Meanwhile, Steve frequently bribed little Sally to read him Dr. Seuss, since he identified with the moral dilemma of the Grinch!

A national survey recorded that the most common male response to the question "What books have you read lately?" is:

"I'm more into doing things with my hands."

Pig-ish things like scratching themselves and playing *Mario Brothers* on their kid's Nintendo!!!

As if that weren't enough, listening to men talk about their cars illustrates without a shadow of a doubt their pervasive absence of intellectual skills.

"You seen that new Porsche?"
"Yeah, vrooom, vrooom!!"
"Ehhhhh! Shift Ehhhhh! Shift Screeeech!"
"Yeah! Pick us up some dumb chicks in that baby!!!"
"First I gotta' change the camshaft!!!"
"Turbocharge, vrooom, vroom, kerbloooey!!!"
"Yeah! Ehhhh! Craaash, booom, vrooom!!!"

They constantly repeat this same mince-meat pie of half-baked ideas in male-bonding encounters designed to *exclude* women. It's a transparent trick to try to fool us into thinking that they know something about anything and that there is some shred of worth in their ignorant toys (which they've purchased with our dress money!).

"You seen that new IBM computer?"
"Yeah, vrooom, vrooom!!"
"Ehhhhh! Shift Ehhhhh! Shift Screeeech!"
"Yeah! Call up some dumb chicks on the modem!!!"
"First install a billion megabyte hard drive!!!"
"Turbo Pascal, vrooom, vroom, kerbloooey!!!"
"Yeah! Ehhh! Craaash, booom, vrooom!!!"

What a hoot! It's as if men expect us to believe they actually use those fancy *mega-ram, mega-Herz, mega-buck* computers of theirs for something more important than playing *F-15 Shriek Eagle* behind their desks all day, pretending to work while they stick women with data entry jobs boring enough to kill a dumb cow!

In fact, the famous spreadsheet program, *Lotus 123*, that men swear they use to build empires and destroy corporate competition, can actually only be used by men in its *secret game playing mode.* Haven't you noticed how men spend their days in corporate role playing games while they leave the real work of running the business to their women secretaries? Yes, we're the ones who puzzle over those endless rows of digitized gibberish (generated by *Executive Mailboys*) every morning before we chuck the reams of useless data in file 13 and go ahead and order 100,000 widgets so the company won't go bust!

"You seen the stock report today?"
"Yeah, vrooom, vrooom!!"
"Ehhhhh! Shift Ehhhhh! Shift Screeeech!"
"Yeah!   Trade a few shares with some dumb chicks!"
"First I gotta' cut up their credit cards!!!"
"Turbo commodities, vrooom, vroom, kerbloooey!!!"
"Yeah! Ehhhh! Craaash, booom, vrooom!!!"

See what I mean? Everything men say to each other is composed of the same intellectual compost turned over and over again like eggshells rotting in the sun!

No wonder women have such an incredibly hard time understanding men! *Their lights are off and nobody's home!!*

Yes, meet the modern man. Retarded, slow, stupid, boastful tree sloths who somehow survived the last ice age unmolested by evolutionary progress. It's not hard to fathom why women love too much, any affection male Neanderthals receive at all is beyond their quota!

7

ALIENS AMONG US

hy the hell are men so weird??!!

Invaders From Another Dimension?

Every woman must ask herself that same futile question at least five times a day (fortunately, hyperventilation usually relieves the ensuing seizures before we can hurt ourselves).

I know this is going to sound bizarre and incredible, but there's only one rational theory I know of that explains male weirdness.

IT'S BECAUSE THEY'RE ALIEN PIGS FROM ANOTHER PLANET HELLBENT ON THE DESTRUCTION OF WOMANKIND!!!!

I know what you're thinking, that Sonya's been hallucinating little bugeyed creatures with green skin and three fingers on each hand (Okay, I admit I dated a guy like that in high school before I got my braces off, but we were just friends!). No, I'm stone cold sober and as serious as I've ever been.

I have inside information from a bona fide alien abductee from North Little Rock Arkansas, one Beverly X (not her real name to protect her from alien rape and the IRS), who gave me the whole story!

"I seen 'em!" reports Beverly. "They're called the ORGSA from the Crab Neb-U-La and they told me everything! Yup, *MEN* are a failed biological warfare experiment masterminded by aliens from a dead planet deep in the Crab Neb-U-La."

Beverly communes with the ORGSA (and with Whitley Strieber, the author of *Communion*) on a frequent basis and has this to say about men.

"Hideous DNA mutates, that's what men are! They were developed by the aliens to multiply like cockroaches, but were just too dangerous for the peacelike ORGSA to leave lying around any old dead planet circling a cold sun. The long and short of it is that the ORGSA threw some dice and as luck would have it, they decided to shuck the whole damn insect horde onto poor old Mother Earth!"

Ladies, I don't know about you, but this theory about why men act like creatures from the Black Lagoon makes more sense to me every time I hear it!

Consider the evidence, oh ye sceptics. You know those chronic migraine headaches we women always get? You always knew those headaches had something to do with the men in your life and now you know why: it's obvious they're a direct result of a male/alien plot to secretly suck our minds out of our heads by hidden probes they insert whenever we're inebriated enough to go to bed with them! Explains a lot, doesn't it.

And why can't men reproduce themselves, forcing women to have babies AND stretch marks?

It's simple, men/aliens are *parasites* and in order to reproduce must deposit their eggs in their victims. (This scientific truth was proven in the documentary ALIENS, with *Sigourney Weaver*). While women walk around barefoot and pregnant, these alien pig-men are male-networking and male-bonding into a giant web, a global alien nation intent only on the humiliation and obliteration of womankind!

Ask me if I'm paranoid!!

Yet, the worst kind of alien pigs are the male Cubans. They're so gorgeous and charming (like Emilio, my grocery boy), you'd never guess that they were really Marielitos from outer space, hellbent on the secret conquest and destruction of the female species!

But can these guys dance the *lambada*!!!

Yet, that's not all there is to this horrifying story! As anyone who has ever ridden in a New York taxi will swear, the aliens are multiplying geometrically. In fact, New York taxis are actually camouflaged teletransporters used by the ORGSA to dump hordes of mutating aliens on our world.

"Nyet! I dun't understud what is this lambada!" Mikhail, an alien Russian taxi transporter recently told me, though I begged him to reveal the secrets of the forbidden dance. "Better to polka and drink vodka till we are falling down drunk, my little babushka!" He smiled as though he were a creature from the planet Zorg.

I mean, if women are going to have to put up with this alien invasion, at least don't make us polka our way into oblivion with aliens who eat potatoes and drink fermented potatoes and think high fashion is a potato sack! I don't care if you're as American as apple pie or an alien from the planet Pluto, you've got to treat your woman with a little style and excitement!

Look, whether the problems women have with men are due to mankind's lack of half an X chromosome, or because male brains have calcified, or because men are indeed aliens from a different galaxy, it really doesn't make any difference because all men are alike (like all aliens) (like Steve and Emilio).

THEY CAN'T HEAR A WORD WE SAY UNLESS THEY'RE WACKED ON THE HEAD WITH REALITY. THEY JUST DON'T LISTEN!

I know one dose of reality that might cure these irresponsible dolts. If they don't treat their women better, we should return them to that planet in the Crab Nebula, even if they didn't come from there!!!!

8

WARNING SIGNS

How many times have you told yourself that your latest beau is an exception . "He's not like the rest," you say. "He thinks of me as an equal!"

Speaking In Tongues

Hah ! !

How many times have you kidded yourself into believing you could spot the telltale phrases of a sexist pig?

Well, just when you thought you'd heard every sexist cliche in the book, out pops another clinker!

The only way to keep from being caught off-guard by silver tongued gigolos is through constant, diligent study, so I've prepared a two step guide for women to take with them everywhere (it's better than mace!). Your first task, as you'll see, is to pinpoint the true meaning of whatever the hell babble men happen to say to you.

PIGSPEAK
A Pig-English Dictionary

CAN I BUY YOU A DRINK?
(Let's hop in the sack.)

PARDON ME, YOU'RE VERY PRETTY.
(Let's hop in the sack.)

I'VE NEVER MET A WOMAN WHO COULD EXCITE ME BOTH PHYSICALLY AND INTELLECTUALLY THE WAY YOU DO!
(Let's hop in the sack.)

YOU'VE GOT GREAT EYES!
(Look at those hooters!)

I LOVE YOU.
(Put me through Med school until I can afford a real babe.)

I'M SO LONELY. MAYBE YOU COULD JUST HOLD ME.
(You'd better do it like a bunny, toots, or it's hasta la bye-bye!)

LET'S JUST BE FRIENDS.
(Now that we've been to bed what else is there?)

I'LL GIVE YOU A CALL NEXT WEEK.
(Good riddance. If you don't kiss the ground I walk on and look like Marilyn Monroe reincarnated, I'd rather work on my car.)

CALL ME AT THE OFFICE. I LIVE THERE.
(I'm married.)

I'M DIVORCING MY WIFE SO I CAN MARRY YOU.
   (When *hell* freezes over!)

WILL YOU MARRY ME?
   (...and be my submissive slave forever?)

YOU'RE PREGNANT? GREAT!
   (Adios amiga, that little bastard can't be mine!)

I PROMISE I'LL NEVER FOOL AROUND ON YOU.
   (At least with anyone you might find out about.)

I CAN'T LIVE WITHOUT YOU!
   (Without you and the kids, where will I get my tax deductions?)

I MISS YOU!
   (I have no more clean clothes. Come over and do the laundry.)

YES, DEAR, I UNDERSTAND.
   (Nag, nag, nag.)

WHY CAN'T I GO OUT WITH THE BOYS?
   (Why can't I go out, do disgusting things and come home smelling like yesterday's garbage?)

HER? WHY SHE'S JUST A FRIEND.
   (She did it like bunny! I hope I didn't lose her phone number.)

NO, YOU'RE NOT FAT.
   (You're a cow! You're a cow! Moooo!)

I HAVE A PROBLEM WITH INTIMACY.
   (I have a problem with intimacy.)

   See, it's not so hard to understand what they're *really* saying. As you begin to develop a working knowledge of "What they say is *not* what you get," you'll then be ready to move on to using some of my favorite come-backs to their transparent come-ons.

TALKING PIG TONGUE

I LOVE YOU!
Sure, pig, where's the diamonds!

I CAN'T LIVE WITHOUT YOU!
Rest in peace! I'll send flowers.

I WISH I WAS GOOD ENOUGH FOR YOU!
So do I!

I CAN'T AFFORD THAT MUCH ALIMONY.
Gee, I'm really sorry. Really, I am!

HOW DO YOU KNOW YOU WON'T LIKE IT?
Put up your house as a performance bond and we'll give it a try!)

I'LL CHANGE! I PROMISE I WILL!
Chameleons change too, but I wouldn't want to live with them either!

YOU'RE THE SUN AND MOON AND STARS TO ME!
You'll be seeing stars, buster, if you don't give me the checkbook back!

WHAT DID I DO?
You name it, you did it!

HOW COULD YOU LEAVE ME FOR HIM?
Trust me, it was easy. I used your credit cards!

YOU HURT ME VERY DEEPLY.
The payback's always a bitch!

I THOUGHT WE HAD A COMMITMENT!
So did I, but Bellevue wouldn't admit you.

SHE DOESN'T MEAN ANYTHING TO ME!
Funny, 'cause you don't mean anything to me either!

DON'T TELL ME YOU'RE PREGNANT!!
   Okay, I'll just send you an engraved letter instead!

WOMEN!!!!!!
   PIGS!!!!!!!

WOMEN JUST DON'T UNDERSTAND BUSINESS.
   Is that why you make us do all the house bills?

*I CAN'T STAND IT WHEN YOU GIVE ME THE SILENT
TREATMENT!!!*
   ------------!!!!!!!

I NEED YOU!
   You and the Seventh Fleet.

*I'M THE MAN AROUND HERE AND I'LL WEAR THE
PANTS!*
   Everyone would laugh if you took them off!

I WON'T STAND FOR THIS KIND OF ABUSE!!
   Then sit down, Big Boy.

WHY CAN'T WE HAVE SEX WHEN I WANT IT?
   I can only fake so many orgasms!

IT MUST BE YOUR TIME OF MONTH AGAIN!!
   Yes, but unlike men, women are only forced to be
jerks once a month, not all year round!!

NAG! NAG! NAG!
   Go to hell! Go to hell! Go to hell!

LISTEN BABY, *THERE ARE PLENTY OF OTHER
WOMEN WHO WANT ME! THERE'RE LOTS OF FISH
IN THE SEA!!*
   So why don't you crawl back into the ocean you
came from.,,you jellyfish, and leave this woman alone!

   Well, okay, maybe of few of our comebacks are cheap
shots. But what's the point of wasting kind words on fork-
tongued male nincompoops? As my dear aunt, Bernice
Bernstein, says:
   "DON'T CAST YOUR PEARLS BEFORE (OR
AFTER) SWINE!!"

9

WHY MEN LIE

This is the singlemost pressing issue on the mind of every woman. Although no unchallenged explanation as to why men are chronic, inveterate liars has clearly emerged to date, the following list of possibilities may shed some light on this age-old question.

If His Lips Move, He's Lying!

Five Reasons Men Lie

1. They're pigs.
2. They don't have anything better to do (other than scratch).
3. Their brain is actually lodged in their crotch and it therefore being exceedingly small and one-track-minded, is simply incapable of differentiating true from false.
4. God put their brains in backwards and so even when they think they're telling the truth, they're telling the reverse.
5. They're *Cheating*.

Reason number five makes up over 97% of all instances of male untruth. Even my baby daughter Sally knows that men lie when they're having an *affair*. After all, how many guys come home in the middle of the night and say truthfully:

> "*I wasn't working late, I was exercising my male python of love with that hot waitress over at Charlie's Grill?*"

Dream on sister!!

When, however, your man comes home and says, "*No matter how hard I work, I'll never be able to pay all your credit card bills,*" this is a dead giveaway that he can't afford his mistress, plus a new pick-up, plus you. Yup, he's lying.

Something has to give, girls! And it better not be you and your credit card expenditures!

You have financial alternatives. This is why the only thing you can do to save your marriage is to go shopping. The more you spend, the more likely it is he'll really have to stay at work to keep from going bankrupt and the more likely he won't be able to afford those week-end business conventions (pleeeez!) in Aruba where he's been taking his sixteen year old secretary.

Sadly, upon finding hubby cheating, many women seek therapy or couple counseling at which point some *male* quack arm-chair shrink tells the distraught female that it's her problem because she *loves too much.*

Give me a break!

It's not hard to fathom why women love too much. Any affection pigs get at all is way beyond their quota!!

Pleeeez! Don't be bitter! Just get even!

Okay, so we all know that if you hadn't gotten involved with the lying, conniving son-of-a-gun in the first place, you'd be a million times happier and twenty pounds lighter. But now that you've fallen to his temptation, why not skip the pathos of hum-drum therapy and make the best of your plight by pretending you've just won **Queen for a Day** and the world's your very own shopping mall?!!?

Buy it! Charge it! Put it on layaway! Buy, buy, buy, until your feet are so sore they won't carry you one step further!

GO TURBO-SHOPPING!!!! VROOOOM! VROOOOM!!!!

Even if this sure-fire antidote to his perpetual falsehoods fails, at least you still have a psychological edge. Because you know he's always lying, that's as good as knowing the truth! Don't let him forget it!

BUT WHATEVER YOU DO, NEVER, EVER, EVER, MAKE THE MISTAKE OF ASKING A MAN WHY HE LIED WHEN YOU'VE CAUGHT HIM IN THE ACT, UNLESS YOU REALLY WANT TO GET AN EARFULL!!!!

"Okay, the **real** *reason I slept with your best friend was because I thought it was the only way to save our marriage,"* he's likely to explain pathetically, his beady little eyes blinking a hundred miles a minute. *"And I lied about making it with the Ringling Brother's midget bareback-rider girls to keep you from finding out about my affair with the high school cheerleading team."*

In the rare event that Romeo decides to trick you by actually telling the truth (for once in his life), the following test should help you separate pig lies from pig truth..

Sonya Steinem's Failsafe Lie Detector Test

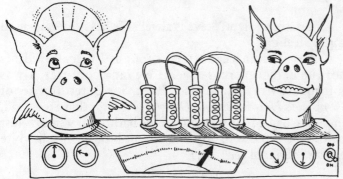

The seven tell-tale signs of male untruths:

1. His fingers are crossed behind his back and his piggy tail is no longer curly.
2. He calls you "Lolita," when your name is "Marge."
3. He has a stupid look on his face.
4. He has a clever look on his face.
5. He says, "I've never lied to you dearest!"
6. He brings you flowers and takes you out to dinner.
7. He forgets to bring you flowers and take you out to dinner.

10

ULTIMATE DECEPTION

Really, my friends, a woman just has to be on her toes all the time. Remember Steve, my ex-husband (please tell me how I can forget him!)? Well, that guy was such a phony, he even faked his own death!!

What a liar! What a pig! Imagine my shock!

Yes, that's right, Steve is alive! He has no regard at all for *my* feelings!

Less than a year after I thought I'd scattered his corpus delecti across several Nevada counties, I was informed by my hair dresser, Pami Sue Burett (owner of *Pami Sue's Hair Salon and Detective Agency*) that Steve had, in fact, wormed his way out of the bathroom window just before the explosion. My hair almost bleached itself white as Pami Sue told the story:

"Just before your house went sky high, my husband Jimmy happened to see your Steve squeeze himself out of this tiny bathroom window, sort of like he was the *Pillsbury Doughboy* and someone had just extruded him out of a square cookie punch. I nagged Jimmy unmercifully and wouldn't even play French maid with him for months until he told me where to find your husband Steve. Turns out, ole Stevie slithered away to some French Monastery high in the Alpines!"

This revelation threw my sensibilities all akilter. Here I had sworn my very existence to upholding the

Just When You Think You've Gotten Over Them!

belief that *Men Are Pigs and Deserve to Die*, but suddenly I was beset by the tiniest yet most treacherous of hopes that perhaps Steve was truly alive. Maybe there was still a chance for reconcillition, maybe the hopes I'd had for our blessed marriage might still be realized, **MAYBE STEVE HAD CHANGED!**

AND IF COWS CAN FLY, WHY OH WHY CAN'T I?

Whoeee, get a hold on Sonya!

Apparently, Steve had become a monk and was an initiate at the *St. Waldo Monastary and Inquisition Wax Museum* under the assumed name Friar Abstemius. According to Pami Sue's great aunt Florence, who was on a whirlwind European honeymoon with a busboy from the Barstow Denny's, Steve refused to respond to questions pertaining to his former life.

"And furthermore," Florence wrote. "Steve holds a silver crucifix in front of him whenever he meets a stray shepherd girl and screams "*Beelzebub Begone!*" louder than the Sound of Music!"

Knowing Steve lived presented me with the anguishing question of whether a die-hard pig can truly be reformed. To find out, I decided to run some carefully controlled experiments on local guinea pigs, which I've presented in the next section. Remember, though, experimenting with pigs is *dangeroux!!*

PART III

LIVING WITH
YOUR PIG

11

CHANGING
YOUR OINKER

Men are not just hard to understand, they're impossible to understand! Heavens knows we've tried, oh how hard we've tried, to figure them out, but the fact is that our only real hope is not to understand men, but to change them!

Old Pigs, New Tricks

Dream On Sonya !!

I know that's what you're thinking, that you've already tried your best to reform your oinker but have failed miserably and there's no way Sonya can help. Let me assure you, you simply haven't gone far enough in trying to exorcise the devils that control your man. You need stronger medicine: neurolinguistic pigramming!

Before you even have a prayer of success, though, you first must try (as impossible as it sounds) to really get inside the pig's convoluted grey matter by conducting a preliminary "getting to know you" interview. As you write down his various responses, note any revealing behavioral or verbal characteristics like spitting and squealing and the like.

I have a brother-in-law, Ralph, who often brags about what a pig he is (Can you believe it, some men just have no shame!). Since Ralph doesn't deny how despicable he truly is (he rather enjoys slopping in it), he made the perfect guinea pig for drastic retooling with neurolinguistic pigramming.

Surviving the initial interview with Ralph, however, was like riding a river raft upside down.

Interview With A Pig

SONYA: Ralph, I'd like to start this interview by asking you something Barbara Walters often asks famous individuals because it really brings out their innermost desires and fears. Okay, Ralph, if you were a tree, what kind of a tree would you be?

RALPH: (Fourth *Coors* recorded at this stage. Ralph scratched himself several times before he spoke.) Hey! You didn't tell me these were going to be touchy-feely questions! (He tried to blow in my ear as I slapped him, urging him to respond to the question). Well, I kind of enjoy hacking down trees with a chain-saw and watching squirrels get squished... Jeez, I don't know. Well, Mickey Mantle was my hero when I was growing up and I always wondered what kind of trees baseball bats are made of?

SONYA: I think it's ash.

RALPH: Well hell, I don't want to be no ash then, because you'd just get made into a baseball bat, but maybe I could be a plywood tree. Does that answer your question?

SONYA: Um, yes, better than you could ever imagine. Um, I always think of candlelight dinners, wine and violins, bouquets of roses as being romantic. Ralph -- what are the things that turn you on romantically?

RALPH: I got your romantic right here, babe! Come to Papa! (He pointed to his crotch and gestured luridly.) Tits, too, I kind of get into harvesting melons every now and then. Hell, though, women all look the same when you turn out the lights. Or when you're drunk enough! (Grotesque laughter, slurping of beer, smacking of lips.) Did you ever hear the story about the transvestite and the hooker?

SONYA: Ralph, you're making me ill.

RALPH: Boy, you women are such teases. First you get me started with all this romantic talk and then it's cold shower time. My offer still holds, Sonya, even if I am married to your sister it doesn't mean we couldn't have a good time.

SONYA: Next question, pleeeez, I don't want to get into a discussion of how warped your morals are. Ralph, if man is the preeminent species on earth, what is it that distinguishes him from the apes?

RALPH: You got me, what is it? Oh, you're asking me? Damn, is this one of those *save-the-whales* questions? Well, men ride motorcycles better than apes, vroooom, vroooom! Did I get the right answer?

SONYA: Well, sort of. . . Lastly, what do you think about male sensitivity?

RALPH: Sensitivity, my ass! I can see why Steve left you, you're a real irritating pain with these questions!!

SONYA: But what about ballet and the opera?

RALPH: Can it, Sonya and get me another Coors.

Of course, during the initial interview you must fight the urge to become excessively nauseous, for with diligent training you can hope to correct a pig's bad habits, no matter how obnoxious they might be.

For example, Ralph benefited immensely by being isolated in a sensory deprivation tank hastily constructed in his garage by myself and his wife Cheryl (my sister). Complete with tow-chain restraints and egg cartons taped to the walls to muffle his screams, Ralph soon adjusted to his new reality and after a short forty days and forty nights of being made to listen to an audio tape of "The Exorcist" played backwards, the results were remarkable.

Neurolinguistic Pigramming had succeeded where all other techniques had failed! Straight after his release, Ralph took out the garbage *for the very first time in his entire life!*

Yes, Ralph's Personal Hygiene and Gross Habits had normalized substantially. Soon, Cheryl and I had visions of taking Ralph to even higher plateaus of Morality, Literacy and Language Skills with additional subliminal suggestions such as "I am the Walrus" and "Paul of the Beatles is really dead", a tape that will either cure Ralph completely or scare the bejeezus out of him!!!

Of course, with lifelong addiction to pigishness, there is a chance the subject will revert to his old habits. Thus, follow-up interviews are required. Six months later:

Interview With A Trained Pig

SONYA: Okay, let's go back to the tree question. If you were a tree, what kind would it be?

RALPH: Nay, I would ne'er be a tree, nor fern, nor bush. Would that I might perchance be a placid pool of water, therein to reflect your magnificent beauty to all the world.

SONYA: Swell. Next, what turns you on romantically?

RALPH: An unquenchable thirst to climb every mountain, sail every sea, ascend every rainbow and conquer that pot of gold so that I could lay myself and it prostrate at your feet, begging only for a second to inhale your inimitable natural perfume.

SONYA: Oh? I'm wearing "Poison."

RALPH: You mean by Christian Dior?

SONYA: No the real thing. Lastly, do you have an answer as to what separates men from apes?

RALPH: (He uttered an anguished gasp as a projectile of pea soup came at me.) Your mother darns socks in hell!!!!

As you may have concluded, this technique does have some odd side-effects. But the good news is that Ralph was so rehabilitated that he has gone to work for me as my slavish publicist. And what's more, using similar methods, I have trained my three sons, Sluggo, Spike, and Scooter to be my copy editors.

But let's not get overly optimistic! Don't get carried away thinking that just because we're women we can always ruthlessly manipulate foolish men into getting everything we want! Sometimes manipulation fails and electro-shock is also necessary!

12

SEXUAL LAST RESORTS

Eating Crackers In Bed

Before you decide there's no way to housebreak your pig, you may want to try some kinder gentler techniques like *three day hysterical screaming fits* instead of letting your oinker turn your life from high-style to pig-style. A good animal training book like *No Bad Pigs* might also work, but remember, these little piggies are greasy, so they may slip out of your control if you don't show them who's boss quickly. Good pig training practise requires:

- Spraying valuable furniture and your lingerie with an environmentally safe pig repellent.
- Hanging a truckload of "No Pesty Pig" strips in your front doorway to prevent piggy buddies from coming over and corrupting your porker.
- Installing an electronic homing device in your guy's navel to keep him from rutting in other women's gardens.
- Teaching him to paw the ground once for "yes" and twice for "no" by waving his wallet under his nose.

Only when all else fails should you consider using the oldest feminine trick in the world to train your pig (and I don't mean threatening to invite your mother on your trip to the Bahamas!). No, every woman instinctively knows that sometimes the only way to show a man who's really boss is to deny him her sexual charms!

Sure, threatening your man with celibacy works, but what about our own need for sensual fulfillment?!? What a dilemma! Let's weigh the pros and cons:

Five Reasons To Have
An Orgasm With A Pig

1. You'll burn calories.
2. It's an acceptable alternative to throwing a tupperware party.
3. You can fantasize you're with Tom Cruise and he'll never know (Tom Cruise I mean. After all, your guy thinks you're doing it with Superman!).
4. It's a break from listening to the constant drone of Ted Koppel's *Nightline Comedy Hour*.
5. You have to have at least one depressing thing to tell your hairdresser about or she won't feel like one of the family.

Five Reasons Not To Have
An Orgasm With A Pig

1. It's humiliating when he makes you talk dirty in French and all you know is "Oui!".
2. You'll miss Stupid Pet Tricks on David Letterman.
3. Don't you already have enough laundry to do?
4. You can't anyway because he's already rolled over and started to snort.
5. It's just impossible to have sex **AND** eat crackers in bed at the same time!

Of course, the biggest reason not to have an orgasm with a pig is that little things add up and before you know it you'll be having them in multiples, not once but many times a day. You'll find yourself turning into a sex-crazed sow, unable to get enough of your man, that swine, which is exactly how women have been enslaved for centuries!!!!

Besides, you just can't give men the satisfaction of thinking they're capable of doing anything right!! If you're truly intent on whipping the old boy into some kind of accomodating shape, then you must be prepared to become the *Ice Princess from Hell* if need be.

As my Auntie Bernice Bernstein says:

"WHEN IT COMES TO PIGS, IT'S KIND TO BE CRUEL."

13

THE END OF THE WORLD

Bigger Bombs Breed Bigger Bozos!

I had a nightmare not long ago that was all too enlightening. I dreamed that some warmongering male had devised a new type of neutron bomb that only killed women, leaving everything else standing as before. In a perversion of nature, the bomb was dropped on America (land of Mom and Apple Pie) on Super Bowl Sunday by President Hogsbrain who had been interrupted once too often by his First Lady.

"Harry! ! ! Can't you stop watching that goddam boob tube for one minute so we can discuss some important matters, like **world peace** and the plight of the **homeless?**" The First Lady had queried. "I mean, how often can you watch the same damn plays run over and over and over again? And come on, don't you think it's a **little weird** for grown men to be patting each other on the rump!"

"**Nag, nag, nag,** Bernice, that's all you ever do!" The President replied, picking up a red phone that was ominously perched on top the TV.

"I'm not nagging," Bernice returned heatedly. "I just think some things are more important than football, your bizarre sexual fantasies and playing tin soldier all over the world!"

The President got an answer at the other end of the line.

"It's started again general," he told the speaker at the other end. "Yup, just as we expected, the nagging just won't end, not even on holy Superbowl day! We're going red alert, general, code alpha, let the bombs fall!"

It was hideous what happened then, for the President had sealed the doom of civilization. Anti-women neutron bombs were soon falling everywhere in the United States (except Utah where women had long since been domesticated) and the screams of dying women tore the atmosphere. It was pathetic, the Super Bowl continued even while thirty thousand women were dying in the stadium seats without even being noticed by their husbands and boyfriends!

At halftime, President Hogsbrain addressed the nation (now exclusively made up of males, plus a few women in Utah, the Playboy Bunny Staff and the Dallas Cheerleaders).

"Boys, the party is just beginning!!!" Hogsbrain announced. But hell hath no fury like that of womankind scorned!

The Super Bowl finished all right, but things began to deteriorate rapidly afterwards. There was now no one to clean the Cheetos out of the sofa after the game and the beer cans were already starting to build up.

"I don't miss women at all," one man was quoted defiantly, as drunk as a pickled goose.

But the next day, beds weren't made, dishes were left uncleaned, and toilet seats had their slip covers removed (to be left standing upright in defiance of all that is moral). Men awoke to a new world destitute of meaning, for there was now no longer anyone left to remind them of what incredibly insensitive stupid shits they really are.

Meanwhile, in Russia, Raisa Gorbachev was telling Puddinhead Mikhail to get up and out of bed because there was a world to conquer, since with the womanly strength of America gone, the Yankee imperialist males would soon be reduced to impotent eunuchs. But did Mikhail listen to his intelligent and charming wife? And do pig stys smell like roses in the summer?

"Da, President Hogsbrain, unleash your imperialist anti-women neutron bombs on Russia." Mikhail was soon politicking over the red crisis phone. "We comrades here in Mother Russia are all unrepentant swineherds too and wish to be rid of the women who give our lives meaning and substance!"

Well, President Hogsbrain was more than happy to oblige and pretty soon the other male heads of state around the world were calling in with similar requests to be rid of their women.

"We never did pay women real wages," some calculating economist chimed on the evening news. "Therefore, women never did have any value and we're better off without them!"

Anti-women bombs were flying everywhere, but chaos was already setting in back in America where this abominable policy had begun.

Ralph Beedle was the first to notice.

"Maggie, I forgot to take out the trash last week and now there are rats the size of Chihuahuas running around the kitchen!"

Except Maggie couldn't respond, Ralph had been too lazy to give her a decent burial after the bombing and she simply grinned at him in necrotic splendor from where he'd propped her up in the den.

"I was going to have her stuffed, but then the ants got to her." Beedle told a friend. Without women around,

there wasn't even anyone around to hide the evidence of mankind's stupidity!

"I can't stand it anymore!" One man was heard to shout just before he pulled the trigger and blew his brains out (his friends didn't even give him a wake, he'd forgotten to leave beer in the refrig for his funeral). "Without women, the entire universe is without meaning and we should end it all!"

Indeed, without women to smooth out the rough edges of the world, men were soon at each other's throats in a bloodbath that made Armageddon look like a kindergarden birthday party. Mikhail Gorbachev flipped his lid completely!

"You American imperialist swine must agree to clean all the dishes in Russia and immediately provide us with clean underwear, or else we will relegate you to the dustbin of history!"

"Listen, you pigheaded Russian truffle sniffer," President Hogsbrain replied. "We're going red alert unless I

see you personally within twenty-four hours, wearing an apron and with a smile on your face serving me breakfast in bed like my (sob!) Bernice used to do! (Oh, what a fool I've been!)."

Well, pretty soon ICBMs were lofting their way out of their silos, crossing the arctic and headed for the anihilation of the lesser half of the human race. That was it, without women around, the whole damn world fell apart!

It would be kind to say that in this nightmare nuclear bombs had destroyed civilization, but it was clear that an even more dangerous weapon had been unleashed on the world: **MALE PIGHEADED STUPIDITY!**

I know, it was all a nightmare. Yet, I get the feeling that it might have also been inspired prophecy.

The only thing standing between civilization and nuclear holocaust is strong brave and clean womankind!

14

LEGAL TENDER

Sue The Pigs!

certainly don't want to alarm any of my more innocent readership, **but there is an insane frightening conspiracy afoot in the land which is the mad handiwork of the global MALE SUPREMACY SOCIETY, dedicated to the annihilation of** motherhood, dolphins and everything that is sacred to womankind!

It's just as we suspected all along! Men's hog-ish behavior is not merely a fluke of Mother Nature gone menopausal! **It's a damn conspiracy!**

My source, who asked to remain anonymous for personal reasons (a certain medical procedure performed by the best surgeons in Tijuana) gave me the documents that lay bare mankind's covert plans for the enslavement of all women. Finally we have cold hard proof of perfidy!

"Sonya," my source pleaded, "Please never reveal that I am Geraldine Bergentramp, formerly Bertram Smythe III of the Smythe herring fortune. It would ruin my reputation as a crack polo player!"

Journalistic ethics which protect my source's anonymity only allow me to say that the heroic process which enabled Bertram to become a sister in our ranks was a phenomenal act of high-tech medical wizardry.

And Geraldine said it hurt a lot! Ick!

As Geraldine reported, there is an age old secret scroll called the **Oath of Male Supremacy** which men recite at male bondings and other equally stupid occasions.

"It was that stupid oath that pushed my switch from AC to DC," confessed Geraldine. "It wasn't something that made you feel light and feathery inside like I AM WOMAN, I AM STRONG by Helen Reddy. When I refused to say the oath, I had my "Macho Decoder Ring" taken away and I was drummed out of the Male Supremacy Society!"

Oath of Male Supremacy

When in the course of male events we find things haven't been going quite the way we expected, we inevitably discover that there was some woman at fault who was nagging us or causing us to lack manly strength at the necessary moment. Since everything disastrous including war and pestilence is the fault of dumb females (Helen of Troy, we rest our case). And since males are by nature superior to the inferior female species, we are drawn to bind ourselves to this OATH OF MALE SUPREMACY.

Therefore, we swear, that it is our manly duty to stand in the way of female ambitions, to keep them barefoot and pregnant, to always make them do the dishes, take out the trash, do the dirty work *and pay them less for it!* This shall be carried out through such devious methods as male-networking, male-bonding, and other incredibly stupid and slothful acts meant to confuse women and drive them completely insane. In other words, treat 'em like dirt boys, 'cause they love it!

In general, males will henceforth act like complete jerks and idiots whenever we're around women and utterly frustrate their efforts towards civilization because this is the only way to keep then in their place, ON THEIR BACKS!

Signed:

Genghis Khan   Attila the Hun
George Washington   Adolph Hitler   Josef Stalin
Clint Eastwood   Ronald Reagan
Margaret Thatcher

Just what the hell were they thinking! ! ! ! !

With this kind of imflammatory propoganda floating around at the highest echelons of public government, no wonder we can't bring the national debt down, at least not before we have a woman president! We've got to fight back on a massive scale and I've got just the winning ticket: the **S.R.A.** (Superior Rights Amendment). This will pay back those cowboys in Congress for not passing the E.R.A.

We don't want no stinking Equal Rights. We want it all! ! ! ! ! !

Yes, you heard me. Why should we settle for less when what we really deserve is **SUPERIOR RIGHTS?** Think about it. More than half the voters in America are female and if we just band together, we can vote ourselves the entire cream puff!!

Therefore, we propose:

THE 27th AMENDMENT

SUPERIOR RIGHTS FOR WOMEN ONLY

Listen up and listen good, you ignorant male slut pigs! Since women had absolutely no say in writing the original constitution, we get dibs on running this country for the next 200 years!

SO WATCH OUT BOYS, 'CAUSE THE PAYBACKS'S GOING TO BE A MAJOR BITCH!!!

We want everything. It's all OURS and you men don't get to keep a damn thing except the bills!! Get it through your genetically underdeveloped thick skulls: the houses are ours; the cars, the kids, all the stocks and bonds, all the gems and gold and natural resources that you haven't polluted already! We want the computers, the fax machines, the mobile phones, and all those toys that you've been spending our facial and nailwrap money on. Everything is Ours, Ours, Ours!!!!

From now on, we can do anything we feel like and you infantile, lowdown, no-good sedimentary creatures can't do anything without asking us first. And you better ask on your hands and knees, because if we feel like it, you'll be sleeping in the garage for the next ten decades!!!

And if you don't pass this amendment you'll be out there for the rest of eternity or until the sun turns cold, whichever comes first!!!!!

But remember, ladies, it's not enough to just change the system at the top. If you really think you want to take a chance living with a pig, you must arm yourself with the following ironclad contract that *GUARANTEES* your personal rights.   Inspired by what that snivelling tennis player did to poor vulnerable Joan Collins, this pre-marital agreement must be signed in blood.

Preferably, lots of his blood!!

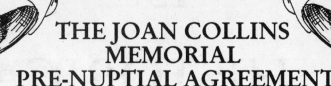

THE JOAN COLLINS
MEMORIAL
PRE-NUPTIAL AGREEMENT

WHEREAS: From before the beginning of time men have been hormonally deranged barbarians lousing up the whole world to the extreme discomfort of all women. And being that men are unhousebroken beasts of the field who require the heavy hand of the law to force them to uphold the miserably few committments and trivial responsibilities of matrimony, and

WHEREAS: *Men are PIGS and Deserve to Die*;

BE IT RESOLVED: That in the case of a breakup of this ill-boding relationship between woman and pig, spawned by the forces of chaos in the pits of a scummy hell, that any children, property, good will, jewelry, artwork, houses, cars, money market certificates, baseball cards or any item that might be of any conceivable positive value shall revert to the aforementioned WOMAN, and

BE IT FURTHER RESOLVED: That any liens, debts, millstones, guilt and emotional baggage that have sprung from this already doomed relationship of convenience, shall revert to the disgrace and dishonor of the reptillian MAN, and

BE IT FINALLY RESOLVED: That the MAN who has refused to give perpetual delight and slavish devotion to the deserving WOMAN, shall legally suffer an eternal fiery purgatory of alimony checks, payments, gifts and appeasements given to the WOMAN at her whimsy, since she is biologically superior and he was obviously an insensitive wimp who should be glad to fulfill the obligations of this contract rather than his real due, knowing as he must that MEN ARE PIGS AND DESERVE TO DIE and it's all their own damn fault!

15

HISTORICAL PERSPECTIVE

The More Pigs Change, The More They Stay The Same!

Call me a kooky cockeyed optimist, but I've often thought the pages of history must hold some hidden thread of sanity to explain how women have survived the heinous acts of their male counterparts through the centuries. Aren't you really sick and tired of that old cliche about how behind every great man there is a great woman!

Pleeeez!!! Smell the coffee!!! Get a Life!!!

The truth is that behind every pig who ever groveled his way to fame or fortune there is a victimized, beleaguered, heartbroken, cheated-on shadow of a once lovely maiden who deserves more consideration than a new Maytag for her birthday!

The only reason there are any allegedly accomplished men at all is that they've been ripping off our best inventions and taking the credit themselves!! Okay, a few exceptions are Sir Isaac Newton (who maliciously discovered gravity just to torment women and make us spend hours wishing we could afford tummy tucks) and Albert Einstein, whose "E = MC^2" was really a sexual innuendo developed only for the purposes of picking up women! ! (It really means Einstein = Male Chauvinist Squared).

So, take a look at history's infamous images and glean what courage you can from some of our beloved matriarchs.

EVE, WHAT WERE YOU THINKING?!?!

Yes, indeedy, when the great-granddaddy of our nation turns out to have been a notorious womanizer and an impulsive spoiler of cherry trees (not to mention a lazy *Mr. Don't Bee* when it came to using his dental floss), it says a lot about the kind of progress men have made over the past centuries.

Zilch!! Diddly / Squat!! Zippo!!

When I search my humble heart wondering how on earth we saintly women have managed to escape extinction through the many millenia of herstory, I am faced with only one realization: It's because we have such a good attitude. We're damned with an *Accentuating the Positive Attitude*, attitude.

Yes, the Huns may be knocking on the door, but we women stand behind our men until the last stick in the village is burned to cinders. And if that isn't a *Positive Attitude*, then I need new bifocals!

But one of the biggest swine of the historical lot was Sigmund Freud because he misinterpreted women's motives completely! Where does he get off telling women that we're driven by **PENIS ENVY** as if men don't have **MAMMARY MADNESS** (they do, but that's beside the point)! Dream on Sigmund, you repressed old dirty bird! If anything, we have **PENIS MOCKERY**, because they're such funny-looking *little* things and because penis is such a ridiculous word in the first place!

But not half as ridiculous as some of the pet names that men call their little beasty! Names like:

Peter the Great
Trojan
Atilla the Hun

I once suggested "*Little Napolean*" to my former husband Steve, but for some reason he was not amused.

BUT I DIGRESS INTO THE ABSURD!!

The real question is why women's place in history needs to be analyzed by couch-potato psychiatrists and explained by male historians who have yet to figure out that men would have been sitting on their duffs picking lint out of their navels for the last million years if women hadn't pushed these momma's boys out of the nest.

And then once we've gotten the old man to take a hike so we can get something done around the house, does he do something productive with his time? Hell no, instead he joins the army or starts a government and jockeys with the other macho-men to see who can lay waste to the greater portion of humanity.

And then they call this history!

Women want our place in history recognized without reference to battlefilds and body counts. History is what you've built and the families that have been nurtured, not how many countries you've destroyed and how much salt you've poured on the fields of the conquered!

Here's another historical perspective for you. How come it's always the men who get to do all the pillaging and raping and burning while we're supposed to be the raped and pillaged and burned? You'd think that just once men would let the women go through the streets of Rome or Paris on a wild rampage, though I suspect we'd probably skip the raping and burning and go straight to the power shopping!

In the mists of time, men used to launch ships in the name of the women they loved, but today you're lucky if you can get your man to launch a coin-operated laundry in your honor much less brave a trip to get you some *Dunkin Donuts*. Somehow, it's not the same.

But perhaps times have changed and history no longer generates men of mythical proportion who stand above the crowd. For example, I know there are many Cleopatra's out there, but where are the Anthonys waiting to throw themselves at our feet?

And imagine if you were Helen of Troy and your king and husband wasn't Agamemnon, but *George Bush!* Girls, you'd have been stuck on that rock heap called Troy until the cows came home before George would have come up with the bucks to pay Arnold Schwarznegger to play the part of Achilles.

And then when George did come to rescue you, it wouldn't be in person, but via some cruise missiles launched from five hundred miles away that would just as likely blow you to bacon bits as win you your freedom.

Where's the heroism? Where's the romance? Where's the movie royalties from the mini-series?

Yes, women may be under-represented in the history books, but I think this is more of an honor than we may have suspected. I mean, how many women do you know who would be as stupid as General George Custer at the last stand? And how many women think the Cuban missile crisis was a grand moment in history? And how many women think it's wise to build fifty thousand nuclear bombs and leave them in Kansas wheatfields?

I rest my case!

16

WHO CARES IF DIETS DON'T WORK!

Let Them Eat Cake!

The first step most misguided women take when feeling emotionally undernourished by their men, is to go on a frantic diet and exercise program. Sadly, all this denial fantasy usually accomplishes is a call to the Maytag repairman to replace the refrigerator door you crowbarred off when you lost the key to the padlock (installed when you thought your diet had a chance).

Call me nuttier than a fruitcake with a banana split on the side and topped off with a chocolate malt, but why should women deprive themselves nutritionally when we're already love-starved enough as it is?!?!

Believe me, food is a fabulous substitute for the understanding, caring, attention and patience that women never get in the real world!!! Has a pan of chocolate fudge ever called you fat? On the other hand, I have often heard chocolate layer cakes calling my name and saying they love me just as I am!

Besides, *Diets Don't Work! !* Diets are totally self-defeating torture tactics developed by male swine to destroy our egos! These tactics must have worked, I think it's time for a bon bon!

Fun Diet Facts !!

1. Men only diet when their coronary arteries are clogged like a *shower drain* or when their twentieth year high-school reunions are coming up.

2. It is a *federal law* that women must live on celery just for the perverse pleasure of morons who aren't even satisfied when we're shaped like a *frigging hour glass!!!*

3. To attract men in traditional mating rites, women are *culturally conditioned* by subliminal television messages broadcast during the *Phil Donahue Show* to worry themselves into anorexia, while at the same time being forced to cook up masterpieces of culinary delights to win over their man's stomach.

4. When your husband, Mr. Lardball, shovels dinner into his bottomless pit, he is required by the *Magna Carta* to comment that you're no longer the svelte kitten he once knew!!!

5. If you scream at your infernal sack of potatoes that women were meant to have a little natural padding of fat because the good Lord knows we carry the entire burden of the galaxy on our backs, *he will be insulted!!!*

6. *COSMO* has printed over *seven thousand articles* on how to reduce yourself to the twig you were at aged 13. They were all written by the *same man!*

7. If women weren't meant to be voluptuous, then God wouldn't have created *chocolate bonbons!!!*

8. MEDICAL FACT: the health of every women is directly dependent on the intake of *enormous amounts of carbohydrates.* Superwomen like my fave, Elizabeth Taylor, have proven this truth time and time again.

9. Chocolate provides a *necessary vitamin nutrient* called endorphins; these natural painkillers are the only reason women have to be able to tolerate insufferable pigs!

10. A little extra heft gives women *extra leverage* when loverboy tries to take the credit cards away. He'll never push you around again once you've passed that magical two hundred pound mark!

It has become all too apparent that low calorie, low cholesterol diets are archaic, oppressive relics of the past. If you must diet, we suggest a high endorphin, high energy plan (basically consisting of as much chocolate as you can humanly consume in one day), designed to get you through the anxiety attacks that confront us all in this male afflicted world. There's nothing wrong with being *Rubenesque!*

So look out anorexia, here comes the unashamed full-figured woman who doesn't care if men don't like the normal proportions that Mother Nature gave her!   And remember, every time a man's eyes bulge at seeing some stick-figured blonde bimbo with big boobs: this woman does not exist! She is a hologram, a trick done with mirrors (*or silicone and liposuction!*), conceiveable only in the twisted mind of a bona-fide male-chauvinist-pig who'd rather own a plastic blow-up doll than learn how to romance a flesh and blood *real woman!!!!*

What About Exercise?

Not necessary unless you're single. If you are co-habitating with a man, then you are automatically burning off so much energy cleaning up after him and throwing temper tantrums that an exercise regimen is simply redundant.

Observe these factual comparisons:

- An hour of kitchen work is equivalant to an all-day mountain climb.
- Stomping your feet and pouting for twenty minutes provides twice as many cardiac benefits as an hour of aerobics.
- Chasing your man around the house and yelling PIGGG!!! is more exerting than training for the triathalon.
- Gossiping on the telephone with your girlfriends for ten minutes a pop will firm up the jaw and chin far better than any damn cosmetic surgery administered by some *Dr. Tinker Bell.*

And speaking of gossip, isn't it odd the way men accuse us of being such jabbermouths, when they're a zillion times worse in squealing every intimate detail of their sexual conquest to their buddies?

Pleeeez!!

But, listen, if you want to let off so much steam that you'll instantly drop pounds of unwanted water-weight bloat, read the next section.   And remember, like Aunt Bernice says:

"NO MATTER HOW FAT YOUR PORKER IS, *YOU'LL* NEVER BE THIN ENOUGH!"

PART IV

ALL MEN ARE PIGS

17

PIG IN A POKE

Up until now we've been talking about the generic failings of men, but the truth is that *Pigs* seem to come in varying styles of piggy-ness; in all shapes, sizes, colors and designer packages. Don't let this frighten you, after all, their mothers can tell them apart, so you should be able to pick out the different makes and models of swine before you mistake a curly tailed one for a real oinker.

But no matter how they disguise themselves, no matter where you find them or how cute they appear after you've wiped the beer foam off their snouts, most men are still PIGS! (Unless its Tom Cruise and he happens to want a date, then I take it all back!)

Just to convince you, we're going to examine the six most common varieties of men and prove, beyond a shadow of a doubt, that they're really *all the same* (remember, the ugly beast called sexual stereotyping is strictly a male disease, *women don't stereotype, we tell it like it is!*).

The Classic Macho Pig

The best way to recognize this slab of beef is by his protruding muscles (especially the one between his ears!).

He and his buddies were the ones telling Jane Fonda Workout jokes while they leered at you doing aerobics, and now he's the jerk standing and grinning behind you at the gym's Stairmaster.

"Listen, you've been on the Stairmaster longer than the allowed fifteen minutes," he belches suavely. "Instead of me reporting you, why don't you give me your phone number," and as he flexes you try not to gag on your Richard Simmons soy protein shake.

If for nightmarish reasons you fall for *Mr. Musclebound's* ploy and give him your number (maybe because you dig his body or because he's a notch up from the plumber's assistant supposedly studying fluid mechanics who last fooled you into a date), you can still try fending him off when he calls you at home:

"Remember me, I'm the guy with the most excellent bod?"

"KhaHackka Kaghhacckk!!" you should respond. "I'm sorry, I just swallowed my cigar butt I'm so happy to hear from you!"

The cigar swallowing tactic should be disgusting enough to dissuade most health freaks from continuing to hit on you, but if that doesn't work, please don't try weak excuses like:

- "I'm already seeing someone," (he won't care)
- "I'm married," (he won't care)
- "I'm schizophrenic," (he won't know what that means)
- "I'm into women," (he'll want to watch)

The best way to get rid of the classic macho pig is to ask whether you can bring your three or more children on the date.

"Oh you've got kids, what a bummer," he'll say just before breaking the date he never got. "I'm allergic to bee pollen and child hair!" And, hopefully, you'll be done with him.

The Intellectual Pig

Sometimes a little easier to reject than the macho guy, an intellectual pig is much harder to detect and can be lurking just about anywhere -- libraries, art galleries, the theater, the grocery store. The problem is that when you meet him, with his glasses and his longish hair and his scholarly, soulful eyes, your heart will really soar as you believe that, yes, maybe this could be that one in a million catch who's studying to be a doctor or lawyer or famous movie critic.

Intellectual pigs have this way of interjecting multi-syllabic words that make you swoon, even in the middle of the broccoli section of the local *Food Mart.*

"I don't want to sound facetious," he'll say, "but I felt an implosion of ersatz erotica when I saw you perusing the cauliflower and I wondered if you'd accompany me to an esoteric, art nouveau film tonight; *Yojimbo* by Kurasawa."

"Yes! Dear God, yes!!" You'll be so tempted to tell him. "I'd love to be treated to a night on the town!"

If he responds:

"Since I could ne'er sully nor defile the alabaster pure independence of spirit that makes you holy in my sight, I'd prefer for your sake we go Dutch Treat," pack him off to Holland!

Intellectual pigs never pay and in the end they tear your guts out just like all the rest. "I'm so sensitive,this hurts me more than it hurts you!" they'll sob as they dump you (usually just after you've put them through law school!). So don't let this cheap strategy succeed, the only reason the bum is crying is that he's just seen the restaurant bill or his new contact lenses are bothering him!

Ugh! Yuppie Pigs!!

Boo! Hiss! We hate yuppie pigs! When one drives up in his BMW or convertible Saab and tries to "pencil you in" his file o' fax somewhere next week, tell him to go perform a tax audit in another neighborhood. You can't even grab a quick cup of coffee with this bore, since he's already been decaffenated and will want to debate the pros and cons of oatbran!

Yuppie pigs are too much of a snooze to even describe!!! But there is one thing you should know in regard to Yuppies, and that's how to get even with them.

Just send them a neverending circular fax with the ends taped together that says:

"Get a life, before it's too late! BMW's cost too much, Bri cheese stinks and Ronald Reagan dyes his hair black!"

Be warned, though, this may cause Yuppie cardiac arrest!

Ken Doll Pigs

Women, the Ken Doll Pig (who has more hair products in his medicine cabinet than you do), is one of the more dangerous, because he's so seductive at first. That perfect hair and golden tan, boyish good looks and sporty clothing hide the fact that this guy was playing with Barbie Dolls before you were.

Ken pigs are sometimes good for a few fun years, at least until they start to go bald and simultaneously realize that the vacuum between their ears is a severe disability in the job market. They are then apt to go into a mid-age feeding frenzy (even if they're only twenty-four), trying to convince women they've still got what it takes, when all they had to begin with was a couple of clean shirts and a head of hair to set them apart from the rest of the herd.

The Married Continental Pig

This oaf is the chronic scamster who (what a surprise!) never tells you he's married but always manages to drop tantalizingly chic names of restaurants, hotels and exotic cities where he's about to take you on your first date so that you're just about to say yes when he blurts out:

"Or we could skip flying to Manhattan for dinner at Elaine's and just get to know each other better *AT YOUR PLACE.*"

If he's shown a bit more restraint and has gone so far as to take you to a dining establishment somewhere other than your bedroom, you can bet your bottom dollar it will be in Nova Scotia and he'll be dressed up in disguise as an Eskimo. Regardless of the fact that this man seems to have money to burn on you or that he's part of the jet set, your dinner conversation will most likely be less than enthralling.

"Arooo, arooo, pant, pant,pant," he'll articulate as he wonders how long it will take him to score. Before you get yourself into that quandary, just remember there is one line that's the sure mark of the married continental pig.

"You make me feel so young," he'll always say, no matter what his age.

The Original Pig

I've saved the worst for last. This is the brilliant so-and-so who's come up with a very unique way to pull the pigskin right over our eyes! He'll tell you right up front that he's a pig. He won't try to say "I'm an entrepreneur," (which translates as being unemployed) or "I'm an airline pilot" (meaning he has five wives on alimony). He'll bluntly tell you he has no job, no car, that he's fathered six illegitimate children and that the last thing he wants is a relationship.

"I only want you for sex and I'm too stupid to have a conversation about anything except hockey and I know you hate sports," he'll unabashedly say. " So I'm warning you, it's best if we don't go out and don't even bother giving me your number, unless you have no self-esteem or you're dying for some male punishment."

Then the inventive pig will add the clincher that nails you to the wall, "You just can't handle an honest guy, can you!?"

"Well, no. I mean yes! I mean no!" you'll answer tentatively before you figuratively hang yourself. "Actually, I like honesty, and I have plenty of self-esteem. I guess it couldn't hurt to go out with you once."

"Don't do me any favors," says the pig until you're literally begging him for a date! Before you know it, he's kept his word and ruined your life.

In addition to these popular breeds, there are other perennials, such as The *Pig Pig* (sure, we all have a weakness for a man in uniform), The *Neurotic Pig* (whose therapist blames it all on you and his mother), and The *Cheap Bastard Pig*, the one we inevitably marry.

But think about it this way:

WHAT WOULD YOU DO WITH YOUR FREE TIME IF YOU DIDN'T HAVE TO SPEND IT WORRYING ABOUT HOW TO GET RID OF THE LATEST CREEP IN YOUR LIFE??!!

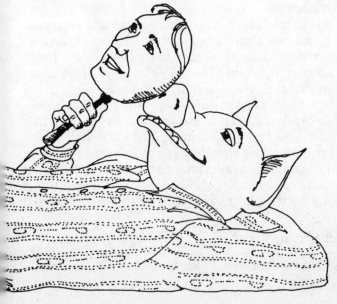

18

THE EVOLVED PIG

Have you ever noticed how men are like flypaper? Once you get caught by one, you're stuck for life.

Old Lovers Never Die, They Just Return To Make You Cry!

Oh sure, old lovers will pretend they don't want anything to do with you, for a while, until they figure out how much they really need you and can't live without you. Then like a whipped puppy they come skulking around with "Oh Babycakes this!" and "Oh Honey, I've been such a fool," until you're half tempted to take them back and even do all the laundry they've saved up since they last saw you.

I was so mad at Steve I threw away the first eighty-six letters he sent me from the monastary. It was the eighty-seventh one, specially marked with a heart shaped cherry Pop-Tart stain that said "*I Love You*" as only Steve could have said it, that threw me into a conundrum.

Perhaps this letter was filled with cold lies solely meant to break my heart? But maybe Steve was writing his heartfelt apology for having ruined our relationship? Or maybe he was writing to say that he'd just cured himself of terminal brain cancer by thinking of me and that he'd never lust after another woman the rest of his life, especially since he'd joined the French Foreign Legion!

Enquiring minds needed to know! ! !

So like a silly ninny, I opened the damn letter and this is what it said:

Dear Sonyacakes,

Time sure flies when you're a monk at St. Waldo's Monastary. I think of you every morning at our thought purification meditation when Father Flatulent hoses down the celibates with water from the nearby glacier lake. Sonya, it's been three years since we met our Waterloo and I miss you.

I'll admit some of the earlier eighty-six letters I sent were translations of "Les Liasons Dangereux" that I paid one of the other monks to copy for me, but I swear that I'm much more sensitive now (really!). Over time, I've become fluent in English as well as French, Russian, Hebrew and Greek. Just thought you'd like to know, mon cherie, perhaps I am not the brute you thought me to be! Again I'm sorry for being such a "cauchon" (little French pun there, would a pig by any other name smell the same!), can't you give me another chance?

During my seclusion I've grown in so many ways. I no longer believe Andrew Dice Clay is God's gift to womankind. I gave up my subscription to Penthouse weeks ago and I no longer think "Women should be obscene and not heard" is a funny joke. I sure do miss the kids and, if you wouldn't mind, please give Sluggo, Spike, Scooter and Sally (sorry I forgot her name the last time I wrote) special regards from their father.

Now, if I could just figure out what I did wrong to make you so mad at me. Was it the bean dip I left under the sofa, or perhaps you still can't forgive me for forgetting your birthday, Mother's Day, our anniversary and Christmas though I was nearly suicidal over my bowling scores. Have mercy, woman! What did I do?

Sonya, may I be struck dead by a thunderbolt if I haven't finally learned to respect you as a woman, mother, professional, and human being. Besides, thinking about you on lonely windy nights still really makes me horny and if you don't believe that I've evol . . . . .

As best I could make out from someone else's scrawl on the charred bottom of the letter, Steve had collapsed while writing, struck either "dead" or "deaf" by a lightening bolt of electricity that had hopped seven feet from the Pop-Tart toaster. My God! Would I ever know if he'd really changed! Could a pig-ish man really evolve into Prince Charming? Could Steve still grow and care and love? Was Steve still alive?

These, my dearest readers, are questions I must leave unresolved with you!

19

UTOPIA

**It Sure
Can't
Get Any
Worse
Than
This!**

While writing this book, there were a thousand emotions and troubling questions that boiled deep inside. Perhaps, in the end, it all leads back to our collective feminine search for autonomy and identity.

Must each woman be all things to all people? Must she be the Nitzchean Superwoman, a homemaker, financier, lover and wet-nurse for the men who depend on her? Or, incredibly, does it go further than that? Is she doomed to be a vassal slave to every man who cares not a twit for her and her feelings?

You better believe it! !

On the other hand, perhaps each of us was instead meant to be an incarnation of *Aphrodite*, goddess extraordinaire of love and Hallmark cards. Surely, we deserve to be eternally worshipped and adored and showered with gifts of tribute from the imperfect men who oink and wallow through our world!

Why of course I am Aphrodite (as is every other woman), just as I am also Nitzchean Superwomen too, but this dual identity is something we've known about all along. Instead, I think what women are really looking for is something much more universal than an identity or a definition of roles.

WE WANT JUST ONE CRUMMY IOTA OF RESPECT!

Women, we know who we are! But do they (the pigs?), and more importantly, do they even care?

For that matter, do we really care who men are and can we ever understand the demons that possess them, demons that often make women's lives more fun than an Exorcism at a hockey game.

Sometimes I feel as if I, Sonya Steinem, and my sisters around the globe, WE together have suffered the amassed male transgressions of millions of years and WE deserve a modest repayment to soothe our ruffled feathers. But the payback's got to be better than men just acknowledging us as mere porcelain figurines (so are toilet bowls and they don't get much respect though they're prayed to every Friday night!!!).

Are we searching for the love of one good man or for the title to a mansion? Maybe we need retribution against the gigolos who've betrayed us; or perhaps an all-expenses paid Caribbean vacation might do? Maybe we're just searching for diamond necklaces, a Ferrari here and there, or a simple card on our anniversary. It is also possible we are searching for the perfect soulmate we lost in a previous lifetime.

YES, DAMN IT, YES! WE WANT ALL THESE THINGS, MATERIAL, EMOTIONAL AND SPIRITUAL FULFILLMENT!!!

Of course, we realize that not all of our yearnings may be fulfilled immediately and complete harmony between the sexes could take a while, so in the mean time we'd be satisfied with something even more fundamental:

WE WANT YOU PIGS TO HOLD UP YOUR END OF THE BARGAIN!!!!

And I guess that's the whole point of this book, *Men Are Pigs And Deserve To Die*. It is not enough for a man to acknowledge that he's a pig (although it's a positive first step). What must happen for our precious planet to survive is for men to also begin a growth process similar to the one women have been undergoing for the past several millennia. Pay heed to your women folk, you may even find they have something valuable to say and much to give!

Ultimately, you see, women would be at a serious loss if the male species expired (who would put up with our nagging then?). So, if only men could be true to their actual pig cousins and learn to be cute, cuddly, clean, well-trained and lovable pals, Mother Earth could relax a little.

Then we could all be friends.

(maybe!)

PART V

LIST OF NON-PIGS

The next six pages contain
a list of all the men I have
known who are not pigs.